DOWN TO BUSINESS

DOWN TO

BUSINESS

The First 10 Steps

to Entrepreneurship

for Women

Clara Villarosa

with Alicia Villarosa

AVERY   A MEMBER OF PENGUIN GROUP (USA) INC.   NEW YORK

Published by the Penguin Group

Penguin Group (USA) Inc., 375 Hudson Street, New York, New York 10014, USA • Penguin Group (Canada), 90 Eglinton Avenue East, Suite 700, Toronto, Ontario M4P 2Y3, Canada (a division of Pearson Canada Inc.) • Penguin Books Ltd, 80 Strand, London WC2R 0RL, England • Penguin Ireland, 25 St Stephen's Green, Dublin 2, Ireland (a division of Penguin Books Ltd) • Penguin Group (Australia), 250 Camberwell Road, Camberwell, Victoria 3124, Australia (a division of Pearson Australia Group Pty Ltd) • Penguin Books India Pvt Ltd, 11 Community Centre, Panchsheel Park, New Delhi–110 017, India • Penguin Group (NZ), 67 Apollo Drive, Rosedale, North Shore 0632, New Zealand (a division of Pearson New Zealand Ltd) • Penguin Books (South Africa) (Pty) Ltd, 24 Sturdee Avenue, Rosebank, Johannesburg 2196, South Africa

Penguin Books Ltd, Registered Offices: 80 Strand, London WC2R 0RL, England

Most Avery books are available at special quantity discounts for bulk purchase for sales promotions, premiums, fund-raising, and educational needs. Special books or book excerpts also can be created to fit specific needs. For details, write Penguin Group (USA) Inc. Special Markets, 375 Hudson Street, New York, NY 10014.

Library of Congress Cataloging-in-Publication Data

Villarosa, Clara.
  Down to business : the first 10 steps to entrepreneurship for women / Clara Villarosa with Alicia Villarosa.
    p.   cm.
  Includes bibliographical references and index.
  ISBN 978-1-58333-354-9
  1. Businesswomen.   I. Villarosa, Alicia.   II. Title.
  HD6054.V55   2009   2009020738
  658.1'1082—dc22

Printed in the United States of America
10 9 8 7 6 5 4 3 2 1

Book design by Meighan Cavanaugh

This publication is designed to provide accurate and authoritative information in regard to the subject matter covered. It is sold with the understanding that the publisher is not engaged in rendering legal, accounting, or other professional services. If you require legal advice or other expert assistance, you should seek the services of a competent professional.

While the authors have made every effort to provide accurate telephone numbers and Internet addresses at the time of publication, neither the publisher nor the authors assume any responsibility for errors, or for changes that occur after publication. Further, the publisher does not have any control over and does not assume any responsibility for author or third-party websites or their content.

For my mother, Mollie Dee Clement Alexander,

who inspired entrepreneurship in me.

In the 1940s, with only a high school education,

she owned a beauty shop; she went on to sell real estate,

and eventually became a broker.

ACKNOWLEDGMENTS

I'd like to thank my village:

Barbara Lowenstein, who casually said to me, "You ought to write a book," and was not discouraged by my reply: "I don't write books, I sell books." She remained persistent and encouraging during the three-year process. And big thanks and much gratitude to Madeleine Morel and the rest of the Lowenstein-Morel crew.

Lucia Watson, my editor, who enthusiastically believed in me and edited my manuscript with a sure hand and careful eye. Her kind words convinced me that I was an author. Much appreciation to everyone else at Avery, under the leadership of Megan Newman.

All of the business owners who candidly shared their stories. They are the future.

My grandchildren, Kali and Nicolas, who thought it was perfectly natural for me to go from being a bookseller to being an author.

My water exercise and gym buddies at the Harlem YMCA, who helped me work out my challenges and frustrations during the writing process.

Elmer Jackson, my superhero accountant, who checked in and sent information and support all the way from Denver.

Acknowledgments

Cisa Mack at Chase Bank, who asked me to do my first workshop, "First Steps to Starting Your Business."

Hue-Man Bookstore, for the experience that allowed me to write this book.

Shannon Ayers Holden, reader and friend, who provided support and honest and constructive criticism, and Jana Welch for her graphic talent.

My daughter Linda Villarosa. Although I never felt like a writer, I birthed a professional writer who patiently helped me understand the technical aspects of writing and editing. Thank you for encouraging both your mother and your sister.

And most of all, I wish to thank Alicia Villarosa. There's no way I could have written this book without her. I am deeply grateful to have a daughter who listened to me and put my thoughts on the page—and who offered lots of tough love through all the anxiety and meltdowns.

CONTENTS

Chapter Ten

STEP 10 • READY, SET, STOP! WRITE YOUR
BUSINESS PLAN, THEN GO!

INTRODUCTION

I was at the lowest point of my life in 1983. After I had worked my way up to vice president of Colorado's largest bank, my manager called me into his office. Avoiding eye contact and reading from notes he had scratched on the back of an envelope, he told me I was *fired*. I was the highest-ranking black woman in the entire bank, and the word was I had pushed too hard, talked too much, and rubbed too many of my white colleagues "the wrong way."

That night, as I cried myself to sleep, I wondered, at age fifty-two, what I was going to do with the rest of my life.

Like many women, I had bumped hard against the glass ceiling. My personality was too big for the confines of corporate America. But in the cold light of day, I also had to admit that I had grown as tired of working "for the man" as he had with me. The very traits that had irked my colleagues—being a pushy, assertive, independent thinker, fast on my feet, with a tendency to stir things up—were the qualities of which I was most proud. And I soon learned that these were the very traits that make a successful entrepreneur. These gifts had been passed down from my own mother, a dynamic self-starter who had run several businesses out of our home on the south side of Chicago in the thirties, forties, and fifties.

So I brushed back those bitter tears, and by the following year I had regrouped and launched what was to become one of the country's best-known independent specialty bookstores. Even though I had never sold a book in my life, my store, Hue-Man, became a small-business success story.

My entrepreneurial flame burned bright, but in 2000, after nearly two decades in the business, I was burnt out. I had served as the first black person on the board of the American Booksellers Association and had become a major player in the publishing industry. I was the African-American go-to girl for agents and editors and had hosted some of the hottest black authors, including James Baldwin, Toni Morrison, Alice Walker, Terry McMillan, E. Lynn Harris, Maya Angelou, Walter Mosley, and Colin Powell. But I was tired. So I sold the store in Denver; I planned to move to New York to be close to my daughters and grandchildren, and coast into retirement.

But before I could book that Caribbean cruise, entrepreneurship again came calling. I was presented with the opportunity to open a bookstore in the rapidly changing hot and happening neighborhood of Harlem. So I got my second wind and opened another Hue-Man Bookstore. It boasted four thousand square feet of floor space and a café, and this bigger and better New York City Hue-Man became the world's largest African-American bookstore. The Harlem store enjoyed the same brand recognition but on an even larger scale, and became a mandatory stop for an author's New York book tour. In 2003, Hillary Clinton chose our bookstore to host a signing for her book *Living History*.

One year later came my crowning achievement. Hue-Man was selected as one of only two stores in the country to mount an in-store event on the release day of President Bill Clinton's memoir, *My Life*. On that warm June evening, the store was mobbed and the signing was covered by local, national, and international media news outlets, including CNN, *Access Hollywood*, and *Entertainment Tonight*. At the end of the day, I had orchestrated the successful signing of 2,119 books.

The Clinton signing marked the complete realization of my vision, to create a million-dollar small business. Now it was time to retire for real, and pursue a new challenge: to teach other women to realize their own entrepreneurial dreams. I now work as a business coach with a variety of clients, including realtors, restaurateurs, retailers, real estate developers, a veterinary hospital, art galleries, and a media production company. I also conduct workshops titled "First Steps to Starting Your Business" around the country to educate, support, and inspire entrepreneurs at all stages of business ownership. It is this urge to give back and use the knowledge that I have acquired that's been my inspiration to write *Down to Business*.

Running a business is full of highs and lows, and somewhere between the fantasies and the ideal—and Cinderellaesque drudgery—lies the reality. The difference between succeeding, breaking even, or being broke is how rigorously you've planned for your prosperity.

Down to Business will draw on numerous sources and existing information that is available but to date has not been compiled and made more user-friendly. I'll take you step by step through the entrepreneurial strategies needed to realize your dream and help you avoid some of the missteps that other entrepreneurs and I have made along the way. This book is full of stories of real women, not so different from you whose examples and information can inspire and pave the way to your success. According to Joy Ott, national spokesperson for Wells Fargo Women's Business Service Program, "women-owned firms are growing and increasing their employment faster than the general market. These firms are driving growth in the American workplace while generating revenues at a similar rate to all firms. This is a powerful statement about the fastest-growing segment of American small business owners." Women own everything from couture boutiques to veterinary offices, wine stores, radio stations, health spas, and ad agencies. We catch the entrepreneurial bug more often but tend to be small, struggle with undercapitalization, realize low revenues, and often employ only ourselves, all of which can hinder potential growth. We often have less personal wealth and lack the contacts to help overcome the hurdles to get the business off the ground. For these reasons, having a good business plan is imperative for creating a successful future.

The businesses I have selected to discuss in this book were not chosen by chance. As you will see, many of them are in Harlem, which is a *hot* and vital community in the midst of shifting demographics. I had a remarkable opportunity to have access to a group of amazing female entrepreneurs in a place that was an incubator for entrepreneurship. This vital community was a microcosm of what was happening in cities, suburbs, and small towns all over the country. This is where I live, am entertained, and shop, so these are dynamic women from my community with whom I have done business. Because I know them and they know me, I was able to sit and talk intimately about their businesses. They were all small businesses and had revenues of less than $1 million and some with less than $100,000. But I also talk about businesses in other parts of the country. Regardless of the location, each one is a success for having taken the plunge and followed their dream.

Down to Business tackles issues and asks questions to help you with preemptive problem solving that will get your business started and maintained on a solid footing.

My purpose in writing this book is fourfold:

- To inform you about the basic essence of business in a way that's easy to understand. This book will "drill down" to make the business concepts quick, uncomplicated, and less intimidating.
- To inspire by my story and the stories of other real women with a variety of business ventures who look and think like you. Each one of us has been where you are and struggled with the same issues. By telling our whole story you get experiences and examples that can help you evaluate your venture to determine if you have a sustainable business model.
- To give you exercises and have you write down your idea and make it real. I want you to gather specific information that you know or researched about your business to motivate you to move beyond procrastination into action.
- To give you a model that you can use to write a business plan. By completing the exercises and specific tasks throughout the book you will have the basic structure, content, and a step-by-step plan that will break down the process and turn it into an attainable goal.

Above all, I want to give you the opportunity to benefit from the years I have spent figuring out the steps in starting and maintaining a successful business. You should never stop dreaming and working toward making your dream a reality.

This book is for you and thousands of other women like you who want to know where to begin. I hope you can identify with the female entrepreneurs in the book, see yourself as a success, and someday let me hear your story.

Chapter One

Step 1

I Believe I Can Fly, but Do I Have the Wings?

ARE YOU READY TO BE AN ENTREPRENEUR?

When I started my first business, I didn't exactly take a rigorous inventory or fully assess my situation. I basically took a deep breath and a leap of faith. But I had several things working in my favor. I had just left a good corporate gig in banking and had parachuted out with my salary and benefits for six months. I was divorced; my children were grown, or at least thought they were, so I only had to figure out how to support myself. To make extra income, I recycled my background as a psychiatric social worker and worked as a therapist part-time. I scheduled one patient a day, which still left me time to devote to the business. Next, I took a hard look at my spending and reevaluated and reduced my expenses. I cut out the extras—good-bye, Ralph; adieu, Giorgio; I will miss you . . . air kiss . . . hello, Target—and lived on a bare-bones budget.

When the time came to assess my direct business experience by the people and institutions that would provide capital, services, and other resources, I really didn't have any! What swung decisions in my favor were the positives on my résumé, which reflected extensive educational and employment achievements with each job, showing progressive complex problem-solving responsibilities. My last position in banking, as assistant vice president of human resources and strategic planning, was viewed positively by the small-business insurance agent, who gave me a discounted rate.

This chapter will help you to determine if you have the right stuff to be an entrepreneur. Reading through and completing the exercises will sharpen your focus and begin the process of honing your idea. By using the list of characteristics and traits included in the chapter, you'll be able to assess your capacity and motivation and gain a better understanding of the reasons why you're thinking of taking on this challenge and how prepared you are.

Before setting off on your new venture, consider the question: Are entrepreneurs born or made? I believe it's both. You're born with certain helpful traits and you acquire or make up for the rest. It's not one rigid set of criteria; entrepreneurs come in all shapes, sizes, genders, and nationalities. Perhaps the one characteristic that differentiates a start-up business, at least in the beginning, is the dramatic impact of its founders and owners. They envision it, create it, and do everything from scratch to get it up and keep it going. That's why it is so important to first understand who you are. This chapter will explore the reasons one decides to open their own business and the personal characteristics it takes to be successful.

Take a moment and ask yourself why you want to do this. Are you giving up a cushy job with benefits and sacrificing your life savings in order to turn your world upside down . . . are you crazy? You need to know your motivation for the major changes you are about to make.

Here are some of the common reasons why people decide to go into business.

1. *Eureka!* You have a brilliant idea and want to give it a try. This idea has been running around in your head, and while you've been preaching like a missionary trying to spread the word, no one else wants to go for it, so why not you?

2. *You're not the boss of me.* You're tired of being an employee with someone else telling you what to do. You've watched your manager and said to yourself, "I can do that, and do it better." You want to call the shots, be a better boss, and assume a leadership role not available to you as an employee.

3. *Ka-ching, I wanna be rich.* You think your idea will make money. You've read stories of entrepreneurs striking it rich and think your idea will be that big cash register at the end of your rainbow. Or maybe it's a way to make extra money to supplement your current income.

4. *I hate my job.* You're uninspired by your work, stuck in a mind-numbing, dead-end situation with no room for growth, and you need to make a radical change. This is often the case with minorities and women who have bumped up against the glass ceiling and feel they can go only so far working for someone else.

5. *You're fired!* Whether they don't need you, don't want you, or are just not that into you; whether they call it corporate downsizing or contraction or outsourcing, you have no job. You may

have been laid off, hopefully with a buyout or severance pay and now you have some money. Even with no money, you see your departure as a sign and an opportunity to shake free the shackles and pursue your dream.

6. *It's glamorous and exciting.* Having a business can create a lifestyle with value, recognition, and ego gratification. You want to feel important and have people, friends, and family look up to you when you say, "I own a business."

7. *Satisfaction, professional growth, and increased responsibility.* You're just not that into them. Your current job is not gratifying and you're dying a slow death punching the clock. You want your work to have meaning and value and not just be something you do for a paycheck.

8. *Flexibility and freedom.* It's about you and your time. You want to work around your own personal and family schedule with more choice in your work hours.

EXERCISE 1 • List your reasons for going into business. By doing so, you can identify the driving forces that are turning your entrepreneurial wheels.

Whatever your reasons, it's important to keep your expectations based in reality. As you start to think about your current lifestyle and what you are willing to sacrifice, you'll need a plan to support yourself in the way you have become accustomed to, since most businesses, at least initially, won't provide enough money to take care of you and your family. If you're married, how does your husband feel about your enterprise? Is he supportive, willing, and able to pick up the slack if it means quitting your day job? Are your friends and family supportive, neutral, or discouraging? Some may be outright jealous because they wish they had the courage to strike out on their own. You may have to let go of some negative relationships and seek out the company of people who are encouraging and helpful. When I opened my store, I learned firsthand about "hateration" and actually lost some friends who were resentful. Understand that not everyone is going to love you for what you are doing.

Tara Simone, a natural-born entrepreneur who, no matter how hard she tried to "fit" into other careers, returned to her true passion.

From the beginning, Tara Simone was fortunate to have the support of her family. She was destined to be an entrepreneur, although it took her some time to realize this. When Tara was a girl, the family's business, Barbara's Flowers, was her playground, and she grew up to adore flowers and appreciate all things beautiful. She spent weekends and summers in the shop with her parents and developed a budding curiosity and a miniature green thumb. By the age of seven, little Tara was her father's shadow, trailing him as he roamed New York's famous flower market. She seemed destined to go into the family business, but Tara wasn't ready to follow that path. As she approached college age, she decided flowers were frivolous and she needed a more "serious" career, so determinedly she marched off to Carnegie Mellon University, majoring in biological sciences and premed. It didn't take long for Tara to realize that medicine was not her passion and that her minor in entrepreneurship was her true calling. Using the family's flower business as her prototype, Tara won Carnegie Mellon University's Enterprise Award and Distinction with her thesis, "Retail Expansion and Product Line Development." Her paper illustrated the successful use of branding from a retail experience, which would eventually inspire her vision for her own career in flowers.

Following graduation, Tara worked as her father's apprentice, learning the details of retailing flowers and styling events. On her days off she showcased her stylish "table-scapes," tantalizing recipes, and floral jewels to a clientele of lifestyle enthusiasts. She wanted to create an environment as a stage on which flowers, food, music, and art would entertain and enrich events and lives. With support and encouragement, she began to infuse her lifestyle concept into the family's business.

Fate intervened again, however, and she married and moved to Maryland with her husband. As a newlywed, Tara strayed again from the entrepreneurial roots. Due in part to pressure and the responsibilities of marriage, she decided to attend law school. Neither the marriage nor the career change stuck. Four years later, divorced and with substantial savings from real estate investments, Tara returned home and went back to work in the family business. In 2006, she opened another Barbara's Flowers in Harlem, with a focus on flowers as a lifestyle concept. As her parents are advancing in age, she has become more involved in the original store. She recognizes basic services are retail, sympathy, holiday decor, urban landscape, event design, production, and corporate gifts. Her challenge has been to outline her concept for the merging of the two stores as she makes her own way in her parents' footprints.

Tara Simone was a second-generation entrepreneur who was blessed with an overwhelmingly positive support system, so fortunately she didn't have to deal much with the envy factor. Although she had regular "good jobs," they were, for the most part, unsatisfying. She saw entrepreneurship as a way to fulfill her passion, provide satisfaction and personal growth, and, as it turns out, earn her a decent income.

First, let's start with a definition of "entrepreneur." *Webster's* dictionary defines it as one who organizes, manages, and assumes the risk of a business or enterprise. My personal definition is one who creates, develops, and manages the sale of products and services in the form of a business. But in my mind, the word "entrepreneur" conjures up a more tangible, flesh-and-blood image. I imagine trying to start a fire from scratch. You begin by collecting a little pile of underbrush and gathering it into a mound. Then you diligently rub two sticks together to produce that first wisp of smoke that ignites an ember. Gently, you blow on the barely lit twigs and add bigger sticks to fuel the flames until you have fire. That kind of preparation, effort, and care make it a good metaphor for the dedication it takes to start a business.

Now that we have a picture of an entrepreneur, let's look at a list of some of the ingredients it takes to make one. First off, *hard work*. It is not a leisurely stroll in the park but more like running a marathon: you train and then it's ready, set, go! Preparing yourself is the get-ready stage.

Read these characteristics carefully and assess yourself against the following attributes.

1. *Self-starter.* You are the one who is starting this business, so it begins with your initiative. Do you wait for someone to tell you

what to do, or can you begin a task without clear and specific instructions? Does someone else have to get the ball rolling, or can you jump-start your own process?

2. *Passion for your business idea.* Is there a burning desire in your gut for the project? This will be something that will consume your life for a long while and you need to feel passionate, not casual, about your enterprise. It shouldn't be something that you can just take or leave. It's more than a hobby, and although it may get pushed to the back burner, it keeps coming back.

3. *High energy.* Do you have the energy and stamina for this race? What is the state of your physical health? Can you work the required long hours, not just during the week but also on weekends? Do you tire easily? Can you go until you drop, and if so, what do you do to rejuvenate? In business there are often no set hours, so forget nine to five—you work when required.

4. *Leadership skills.* It's one thing to be a good manager, but another to be a good leader. Managers know how to do things right, but leaders do the right things. As an entrepreneur, you will be called on to do both. Successful business owners understand that other people are looking to them to call the shots, make the hard decisions, and have the right answers, often on the fly. You set the tone and direction for the business, and people will expect you to take charge. If your comfort zone is about having others tell you what to do, then entrepreneurship may be challenging. To run your own show you need to be an assertive but flexible decision maker.

5. *Interpersonal skills.* As a small business owner, you must be able to establish and maintain cordial relationships with everyone

who touches your business. If you thought getting along with your boss and coworkers was tough, wait until you have to deal with suppliers, lawyers, accountants, government officials, salespeople, advertisers, technicians, landlords, and, above all, customers. All of them want a piece of your time. To be successful, you'll need the ability to work with all types of business personalities, many of them difficult. Included in those interpersonal skills is the ability to give "good phone." Small business owners spend a lot of time talking with people they may never meet face-to-face, so it's important to have a concise, clear style of verbal communication.

6. *Organizational skills.* The ability to keep track of everything happening in your business; and believe me, it's a lot of stuff and requires an orderly system. You'll have to prioritize and get things done without getting bogged down. Multitasking is a good thing but not at the expense of efficiency. You can't afford to spread yourself too thin, get scattered, and lose control. It's like being a busy mom, particularly those who work outside of the home. You have to manage kids' school schedules and extracurricular activities and keep the house together, all while trying to have a career. Being an entrepreneur also means juggling a lot of balls.

7. *Management skills.* The first person you have to effectively manage is *you,* so take a look at how well you structure your time and manage yourself as you handle numerous daily tasks. Now move to the management of others, which is quite complex, particularly if you have employees. Each one has "eccentricities" and can work your last good nerve. With the

management of staff come the functions of human resources. Can you hire, reprimand, and fire employees, as well as compliment and motivate? Are you comfortable assigning tasks and authority to someone else and appropriately monitoring their performance?

8. *Intelligence.* This goes beyond IQ tests. A true measure of intelligence is more than book smarts; it's also street smarts and common sense. Are you pragmatic? Can you deal with real-life experiences and find creative ways to apply what you know?

9. *Problem solving.* What happens when you are faced with a crisis? Do you "melt down," or can you shift out of panic mode to examine the situation and then come up with a solution to work your way to a resolution. Owning your own business is not a static job and is full of the unexpected, like a power outage or a supplier's truck breaking down. Once, at the bookstore, the entire staff was out with a nasty flu bug the week before Christmas, the busiest time of the year. Entrepreneurship can be unpredictable, so how well do you deal with change and uncertainty?

10. *Self-confidence and optimism.* You must believe in yourself or it will be impossible to convince others to be a part of your dream. Your attitude is an essential part of why customers or clients choose to purchase your product or service. If you are upbeat, hopeful, and passionate, you'll find that your enthusiasm is contagious. People are drawn to the light and not to the dark. You represent your enterprise, so it's important to present yourself as a positive reflection of your business.

Connie Perez, who forged a lifelong path to entrepreneurship, has all the ingredients and is the perfect example of what it takes to be successful.

Connie Perez has come a long way since dropping out of high school at sixteen and taking her first job cleaning hotels in Colorado. Throughout her life she has demonstrated all of the characteristics of an entrepreneur, and she has come full circle to owning her own business, Immanuel Cleaning Service. "Immanuel" means "God go with you," which reflects Connie's faith and spirituality.

Connie has never been afraid of hard work. Even as a teen, Connie was self-sufficient when she quit school to work in order to support herself after leaving home to escape a troubled household. Eventually she earned her GED, and after struggling through a series of unskilled, low-paying, dead-end jobs, Connie decided to improve her situation by going back to school. She attended Red Rocks Community College Certificate Program for front-office medical work, which gave her top-notch training and guaranteed employment.

The following are examples of her capacity for entrepreneurship, the path she took, and her timeline to owning and operating a successful business.

- *Throughout the time spent working in medical offices, Connie was able to increase her job responsibilities. She upgraded her certification from medical office to eventually become a medical assistant, with credentials from the American Association of Medical Assistants.*
- *While still working in the medical field, Connie applied for a $5,000 grant from the Mile High United Way for a down payment toward home ownership. When the grant was finally approved five years later, she had already purchased a home and was offered an opportunity to use the money for education or opening a business. She chose the latter.*

- *She continued to raise capital to start her business and added another $5,000 by withdrawing from the 401(k) she contributed to while working in hospitals for ten years. She used this to pay for start-up costs of marketing materials, brochures, business cards, and cleaning supplies and equipment.*
- *As Connie was preparing to launch her business, she attended a workshop at a Women's Resource Center to develop a business plan, learn how to design a website, and register as a corporation.*
- *Once the business was up and running, she recognized the need for more assistance and enrolled in a Denver Small Business Development Center workshop on finance. She also studied resource materials from the library and bought books to learn about managing the finances and cash flow.*
- *In order to increase her client base, Connie initiated a relationship with contractors to learn the bidding process for postconstruction cleanup, which pays better than house cleaning. When she learned that she needed to read blueprints in order to accurately bid on uncompleted construction projects, she located an architect to teach and mentor her on the process.*
- *She became certified as a WMBE (Women and Minority Business Enterprise) and DBE (Disadvantaged Business Enterprise) in order to qualify for special consideration to do business with city agencies.*
- *For a steady income, Connie got a flexible well-paying day job as an on-call delivery person for hospital supplies to pay herself (after hiring employees, she could not afford to draw a salary).*

Connie has shown that she is persistent, organized, high energy, and has natural intelligence. She is a self-starter, problem solver, and takes initiative. Connie has maximized available resources and formed strategic *alliances to enhance her capacity to operate and grow her business. In the first year the revenues were only $25,000, but—to judge from the first quarter of the second year—she is on target to boost that to $100,000.*

Connie is clearly a self-starter. She proved this by having to support herself at such a young age and then systematically working to improve her skill set to increase her marketability. Connie has what it takes: she's an optimistic high-energy go-getter who can problem solve and make critical decisions, the very characteristics that have enabled her business to thrive.

To determine your capacity for entrepreneurship, begin with an assessment of who you are. Compose an expanded résumé or a personal and professional inventory. This will help to determine if you have the necessary tools, both emotional and physical, to be an entrepreneur. This is your personal "Come to Jesus" moment and should be an honest and rigorous evaluation. Include your education, personal history, job history, and the skills and weaknesses that you have demonstrated in each area. As you look at your résumé, do you see technical skills, increasing job responsibility, and managing other people? In your jobs, did you tell other people what to do, or were you told what to do? Do you have passion and "fire in your belly" to go after what you want even if it seems scary and difficult? Compare and contrast your résumé with the requirements for being an entrepreneur.

Here is a résumé for you to review. Examine it for entrepreneurial qualities.

EYE M. CAPABLE
1234 Hire-Me Street
Eagertown Valley, NY 10842
Home phone: (718) 555-5555

OBJECTIVE/SUMMARY

Seeking challenging supervisory position in a community-based social work program with strong outreach component and which requires strong commitment to meeting needs of underserved populations such as homeless and homebound seniors.

Excellent program planning skills and organizational skills. Documented success in grant work obtaining funds to design high-quality, cost-effective, and comprehensive service offerings.

Skilled in coalition building and community support and creating interagency partnerships.

WORK EXPERIENCE

Program Supervisor/Senior Case Manager,
Paul J. Cooper Center for Human Services, Bronx, NY, 4/1996–Present
Progressed through a series of promotions culminating in responsibility for community outreach programs and hospital intake referral program. Supervise a team of ten caseworkers, case managers, and support staff. Develop and maintain strong community alliances with local agencies and state funding organizations.

PROGRAM CONTRIBUTIONS .

- Demonstrated outstanding case management with large caseloads as evidenced by repeated promotions.
- Successfully advocated with federal housing authorities to create low-income housing within the community.
- Provided support services for at-risk seniors that kept 100 percent of clients housed with zero evictions.
- Developed and delivered a presentation that won a $50,000 grant to provide on-site services in a senior facility.

Social Worker/Senior Case Manager,

Services for the Underserved, Brooklyn, NY, 8/1991–2/1996

Served on interdisciplinary team to provide case management for consumers housed in three community group home residences. Developed weekly group programs and maintained case files. Assisted in researching funding sources.

PROGRAM CONTRIBUTIONS

- Designed and implemented creative group programs benefiting mentally retarded consumers and enhancing their independent living skills.
- Launched ongoing agenda that included off-site outings, participation in community events, and group discussions.
- Facilitated supportive services and counseling for clients and interactions with family members.

- Forged community connections and collaborated with team members on development and appropriate case planning to meet clients' individual needs.

EDUCATION

Adelphi University, Garden City, NY, M.A., Social Work
Brookdale College, New York, NY, B.A., Sociology
Greybrook Center for the Treatment of Addiction, New York, NY
CAC Certificate, Certified Alcoholism and Substance Abuse Counselor

INTERNSHIPS

Paul J. Cooper Center for Human Services
Federal Employee Counseling Services, on-site counseling program for federal employees

AFFILIATIONS

National Association of Social Workers

SKILLS

Case management	Community outreach
Intake and direct patient care	Health care education
Data collection and clinical research	Grant and proposal writing
Managing and organizing staff	Record maintenance
Public speaking	

The above is an exhaustive résumé to give you a basic idea. Note Ms. Capable's entrepreneurial assets. Under "Work Experience" she indicated she had been steadily promoted, including work in a supervisory role, which is a necessary skill in order to coordinate staff and monitor and supervise employees of the business. Under "Program Contributions" she has created and facilitated internal and community programs, which reflects organizational, problem-solving skills and marketing. She has also worked with a large multidisciplinary team, which could be similar to dealing with the numerous vendors and suppliers that provide products or services to your enterprise. Your résumé may be less detailed, but make sure it lists all you have done and gives a good indication of all you can do so you know what you have and can access when needed.

EXERCISE 2 • Complete a résumé. It will help you to review your work history and take stock of your assets.

While your résumé may be a good example of your capabilities and talents, do you have business savvy? Or are you a neophyte when it comes to small-business information?

Do not despair. There are multiple sources for information in your own area, and most of it is free or available for a nominal cost. Connie Perez, whose story you read in this chapter, availed herself of workshops in Denver.

Below are ideas for business development services and networking opportunities.

- The Small Business Administration (SBA) is a federal government agency that offers a variety of information, workshops, consultation, and mentoring for entrepreneurs. SCORE is a group of retired businesspersons who volunteer their time and expertise. Small Business Development Centers (SBDCs) are located in states with community offices. To find them, Google the SBA site and click on the locator to insert your city and state. These are among the workshops offered by an SBDC:

Creating a Targeted Business Plan
Techniques in Marketing Strategy
Effective Internet and E-mail Marketing
Financial Management and Financing Your Business
Selecting the Best Legal Structure for Your Business

- Your local county and city may also have economic development offices in your community. You can go to your local government website and look for small-business assistance. Type in your city or state followed by .gov.
- Private not-for-profit programs started to contribute to the public good. They support and develop entrepreneurial small business in underresourced communities. They often target special groups such as women and minorities. Again, you can Google small-business assistance and insert your city or state to get a list for your area.

By talking with professionals and other entrepreneurs, you will drill down to enhance your fund of knowledge and find other resources.

EXERCISE 3 • List your assets and liabilities. Be (brutally) honest. Yes, it's rough, but by completing this rigorous inventory, you can save yourself time by not entering into a venture ill-prepared.

Of the ten characteristics listed for entrepreneurship, how many do you possess or have demonstrated?

Using the ten characteristics for preparedness, for each one, rank yourself on a scale of 1 to 10, with 10 being the best. If your total score is 50 or lower, or if you are below 5 in more than two areas, consider doing something else.

List at least two community resources in your area providing assistance for small businesses.

How many, if any, have you contacted?

Congratulations! By putting pen to paper and completing the exercises, you've taken the first step to turning your dream into reality. Keep your work together in a notebook, and get ready to add your exercises for the following chapters.

Chapter Two

Step 2

Now Name and Claim Your Dream: What Is Your Business Idea?

I grew up in a household where it wasn't just a slogan; reading really was fundamental. And when I had my own family, one of the greatest joys of motherhood was reading to my daughters. As an avid reader, I spent lots of time browsing bookstores, but in Denver there were no African-American bookstores. Denver was home of the Tattered Cover, the largest independent bookstore in the country. During a visit to the Tattered Cover, I got the idea for the Hue-Man bookstore. I began to visualize creating a smaller specialty store with my unique spin. As I planned the design of Hue-Man, I did lots of research. Wherever I traveled, I sought out African-American bookstores and made it a point to speak with the owners or their staff about the business. I got ideas about what other people were doing—the good, the bad, and sometimes the ugly. I tried to figure out what they were doing right so I could incorporate it into my business idea.

. . .

The goal of Step 2 is to come up with a thoroughly researched tangible business idea that will move you forward from the casual to the concrete. This chapter will discuss the importance of external factors, the state of your industry, and how these external factors can impact your business. It will explain the different kinds of entrepreneurial businesses and the benefits and downside of each type of enterprise. Once you've gotten a handle on your concept, the exercises will take you through the ABCs of pricing so that you can begin to estimate sales volume and income potential.

DEFINE AND REFINE YOUR BUSINESS IDEA

Although you may have had your entrepreneurial inspiration for a while, you'll need to *define and refine your business idea*. What exactly will you do? Finding the right idea can be easy, especially if you've been nurturing it for a long time. Or you may have only recently experienced your "aha" moment.

Your original business idea can be inspired from:

1. *A passion*. A yearning that comes from deep inside of you. You look forward to doing it and it brings you joy and satisfaction.

2. *A hobby or special talent*. Something you're already doing for yourself or for friends and family: "Girl, you make the best dog sweaters, ginger cake, and bottle-cap art. You should sell those." Now you're ready to take it to the next level and get paid for doing it or selling it to others.

3. *An opportunity or gap in the marketplace*. You fill a niche by bringing a specialty that relates to a particular product or service or to a specific group or demographic. For example, you can

take advantage of your neighborhood's "stroller explosion" by opening a mommy-and-kids yoga studio.

4. *A bargain.* You can offer something at a better price or more conveniently than anyone else.

5. *A solution or improvement.* Anything you can do, I can do better! Make something bionic, i.e., better, stronger, faster. Think Starbucks and how they've brought sexy back to coffee.

Evaluate your business to see if it meets one of people's basic needs:

Food: Can you eat it?
Shelter: Can you live in it or with it?
Clothing: Can you wear it?
Transportation: Does it get you from point A to point B?

Or is it a discretionary product or service that is purchased after basic needs are met? Do people buy this product or service when they have extra money, say, for entertainment, eating out, or personal services?

Begin to flesh out your business idea and think about it in as much detail as possible. Define it as a product or a service. If it is a product, how much do you know about the product? Is your business idea part of a larger industry? As a bookseller, my product was books, but with a strong service piece. I was part of the retail industry and had to learn all of the marketing components required to get books from the point of shipping and receiving to the shelves and finally into the hands of the readers. Or are you a service defined as providing a benefit to a client that may or may not be product-related. Some examples of services are computer specialist, financial adviser, house cleaner, personal coach, publicist, and event planner. Your "product" is your knowledge, experience, and time that you give to your clients. If you're a personal coach, you define what you will offer clients, and create a strategy to accomplish the stated outcome and a way to measure success. A financial adviser discusses all aspects of the client's money matters and develops a program to achieve their financial goals. The services and fees charged are dependent on the entrepreneur's education, training, skills, and experience and also help convince the client of their capacity to deliver the service.

McEvoy Consultants LLC represents a service business that uses its owner's education and specific skills to deliver a service. Dr. Marcia McEvoy honed and applied these skills in her previous job, and has taken what she learned so that, instead of doing the job for someone else, she works for herself.

Marcia came to entrepreneurship later in life, after a job correction left her devastated and thrown out of a fifteen-year comfort zone. Once she picked up the pieces, she realized she could have a home-based service business consulting for school districts on crisis response, suicide prevention, bully-proofing schools, and preventing abusive dating relationships. She conducts workshops in schools and at the district level with staff, students, and parents. This is a far cry from the young adult who dropped out of college after three years to go to New York to be a professional ballerina. She had studied ballet since she was five years old, and became a principal dancer in the Grand Rapids Civic Ballet Company. In New York she danced in theater productions off-off Broadway and worked as a waitress on the side. But when she was finally getting a foothold through an opportunity at a major ballet company, homesickness washed over her like a flood. She did not love New York; she really missed Michigan. She returned there, completed college, and was offered a full scholarship to the University of Cincinnati for gradu-ate studies in school psychology. She married a classmate from Grand Rap-ids, and after completing their education in Cincinnati, they both returned to Michigan to be close to their families.

Two daughters later, Marcia was a licensed Ph.D. psychologist, working part-time (thirty hours per week) in community mental health and earning a maximum $23,000 per year. She was a liaison responsible for developing and implementing behavioral prevention programs in public schools. In 2001, the state of Michigan reduced the non-revenue-generating departments, and this meant layoffs. After fifteen years Marcia was let go. When six weeks of unemployment insurance expired, she needed to replace her income, and she thought, Why not go for it on my own? The prevention services she had developed for community mental health were well received in the schools, and she was occasionally hired by school districts outside the county, for which the agency she worked for was reimbursed. She struggled with setting up her busi-ness and, like many new entrepreneurs, initially undercharged because she did not value her services sufficiently. Her basic daily rate of $600 has evolved into $1,200 for staff training, $850 for student presentations, and $450 for a ninety-minute parent group session; her rates include travel expenses. She was motivated to make more money to supplement the family income, save for college for her two daughters, and reduce credit card debt. Marcia also needed to plan for her retirement and is thinking about renovations on the family home. Her first year's annual revenue was three times her previous salary. Since then, her annual revenues have been: $117,000 in 2005; $90,000 in 2006; $63,000 in 2007; and $90,000 in 2008.

The work is seasonal, and heaviest during the beginning and middle of the school year. Revenue fluctuates because of Michigan's depressed econ-omy and the continued reduction of state aid to schools, which account for ninety-five percent of her business. Marcia's main expenses are for travel, equipment, and continuing education and professional certification. The only marketing materials she needs are business cards. She does not advertise, and all referrals result from her clients and word of mouth.

Marcia is passionate and committed to her work, and she would like to increase revenues to gain more consistency by market penetration outside Michigan. She would also like to expand her business beyond schools to reach youth-serving agencies including child-care providers, Girl Scouts and Boy Scouts, and summer camps for children. Her goals are to develop more business savvy and to create a website and marketing materials.

Marcia had a very specific and marketable skill set. Her challenge was to find a way to take her valuable talents and turn them into her own business. After she packaged her services and made the entrepreneurial leap, her next problem was pricing. Marcia had to find the confidence to charge the appropriate market rate for her services and earn enough to support her lifestyle and create a viable business.

EXERCISE 1 • Clearly and concisely state your business idea, then elaborate. Doing this will take your original general description and polish it up. For example, I plan to open a Pilates studio. The studio will be in a freestanding space that I will rent. I will hold mat work classes and private and semiprivate sessions on the Reformer machine.

> Break it down in plain language and detail, and then flesh it out in greater detail. Spend time with this task because it is important for another person to really get it. Just because you have lived with the idea, you cannot automatically assume the reader will know as much as you.

Next, think about the state of your industry. Take a hard look at the stability and longevity of your industry. Everyone wants to jump on the bandwagon of the hot, new trend, but typically by the time you're hearing the buzz, it's already "so five minutes ago." Determine whether your industry is growing or shrinking, and where. Is it doing well in collective settings like shopping centers, strip malls, and retail centers, or are freestanding establishments and individual stores driving the market? What are the trends and developments? You certainly do not want them on the list of things vanishing from America like the Yellow Pages, movie rentals, or bowling alleys. How do national and local economic conditions impact the industry? Will the severe economic downturn that began in 2008 influence your business?

If your business is a service, one of the first things to consider is who will provide the service. Will it be you alone, or will others deliver it? How will you control the quality and consistency, and what is your direct experience in the business? For example, a person who likes to cook and is considering opening a restaurant might start with a catering business. It's a smart first step since a love for food isn't the only requirement. Everyone appreciates a good meal, but it's the details of how the food gets to the table that interest the businessperson. By taking a first step into catering, the budding entrepreneur will learn about the issues related to cooking as a business and the food-service industry, but on a smaller scale. There is experience to be gained relating to procurement of goods, the ability to work with distributors and to experiment with recipes and menus without a huge investment.

Even though she had an abundance of passion and determination, Celeste Beatty was still bedeviled by factors outside her control.

When Celeste founded the Harlem Brewing Company, she learned the hard way about how external forces related to her industry impacted her business. Starting her own brewing company has also taught her a lesson about how her product is part of a larger beverage industry whose shifts can mean the difference between success and failure. Celeste's affection for ale and brewing beer began in the early 1990s when a friend gave her a home-brewing kit. Using her apartment as her test kitchen, she learned the nuances of combining water, hops, and barley with flavoring to concoct some outstanding brew. Her "homemade hooch" was a hit with friends and family, and this planted the seed to start her own beer company.

After graduating from college, Celeste worked with Ben & Jerry's in Harlem. Although an entrepreneurial effort, Ben and Jerry provided significant community service and promoted social outreach programs. Raised in a family that encouraged spirited discussions about political activism and cultural diversity, Celeste was inspired by Ben & Jerry's philanthropic business model, and it became her blueprint. In 2000, she and two partners established Mojo Highway, a beer company. Good press and a favorable reception put Mojo on the map, but they lost their Mojo, literally, when two years later their contract brewing partnership ended abruptly. The brewery's stock crashed and their business also went belly-up since there was no way for them to brew their beer.

Celeste's original investment of $50,000 was long gone, but she was determined to create a successful beer in Harlem. She set out again, raising $100,000 from assets in real estate, stocks, heirlooms, and inheritance, and in 2000 relaunched. Her strategy was to evoke Harlem's heyday during the 1920s Renaissance, when beer was the drink of choice of musicians and artists and the standard beverage served at the swankiest restaurants. Her logo includes musical instruments, and her signature product, Sugar Hill Ale, is meant to represent the sweet life of Harlem. Finally her hard work is beginning to bear fruit. Although she's burned through most of her assets and it's still a struggle, sales and name recognition are up. So life is indeed getting sweeter for Celeste.

Celeste's story is a perfect case of something outside specific business operations causing someone to lose almost everything. It's a wake-up call to never forget that your business doesn't operate in a vacuum and there are those often unpredictable external influences that you have to try to anticipate and plan for. Her story demonstrates that you should always have a contingency plan, and for something as important as making your product, get a backup.

EXERCISE 2 • Evaluate how well you're prepared to deliver the product or service, and take into account external factors that you need to consider.

- What experience do you need to deliver the product or service? Do you need to have touched, worked with, or have had some other hands-on relationship with it?
- What are your particular qualifications to deliver the product or service?
- How much do you actually know about the business, and where did you learn what you know?
- Are there any registrations or certifications required for your industry, product, or service? This is particularly important for the food industry.
- Is there any special training or education that you have or need to acquire? If so, list your credentials.
- What is the state of the industry?

ALTERNATIVE PATHS TO ENTREPRENEURSHIP

Although owning a business might be your dream, that doesn't mean you have to start it from scratch. There are other options, like purchasing an existing business, partnering with someone in business, and buying a franchise or entrepreneurship through direct sales. To find out more about these options, go to the library, bookstore, or online to get detailed information about the pros and cons. Here's a brief description to help you determine if one of these entrepreneurial choices might be the right fit for you.

1. *Purchasing an existing business.* Someone has already started a business, wants to sell, and you have decided to purchase since this saves not only the upfront costs but also the business has ready-made customers, reputation, cash flow, staff, and operating systems. Your due diligence starts with getting as much information as possible about the business, particularly the finances, since bad books equal bad business. One sure sign that they're serious about business is if the owners have compiled a prospectus that includes complete information about the enterprise, its founders, the product, and market. You'll also want to know why they are selling and the appropriateness of the price. The price is usually a multiple of the gross sales or the seller's discretionary earnings. Have an accountant review past and recent financials, and above all, be on the lookout for the unseen: whether the employees are committed to staying with the business, and whether customers will be loyal to a new owner. Make sure the seller signs a "noncompete" agreement and accounts for receivables from customers who owe them money. Ask yourself what you will bring to the business and what is the potential to sustain and grow the business. Also determine the owners' willingness to consult with you after they sell. Be forewarned, this can be a long process. With full disclosure and a business broker, it took two years to sell the Hue-Man in Denver.

2. *Partnering with an existing business.* In addition to getting all of the pertinent information as mentioned above, find out everything about this person with whom you'll be working and if you're compatible. Partnership is like marriage, and you best know with whom you are getting in bed. Determine what you bring to the

table, like money and expertise. What is the value of the business, and how is it expressed in your percentage ownership?

3. *Franchises.* You are purchasing someone else's formula for success, which is defined as an arrangement in which you pay an initial fee and sales royalties for the permission to use a trademark product or service with a proven operating system, consumer packaged market, training, marketing, advertising, and ongoing support. This saves you valuable time and minimizes risk by utilizing the franchise brand, its national reach, site selection, developed methods, and operating systems. The downside is the amount of money you're required to put upfront, your ongoing obligation to the business, and loss of control since you're obligated to adhere to their standards and way of doing business.

4. *Direct selling.* So you don't have a truckload of money and have no desire to spend long hours managing a big business with employees? Then consider something smaller, something home-based, like selling nationally branded products or services face-to-face without a retail location. We all know about the Tupperware model or the Avon lady. Signing on as a sales consultant or independent contractor for a particular brand in a territory can be a stepping-stone to entering the world of small business. You start with minimal capital (cost of the products), a network of potential customers, and good sales skills. The more personality you have, the better, and by recruiting sales representatives, you can add to your compensation.

But buyer *beware!* When purchasing, partnering, or franchising, don't sign *anything* without consulting an attorney. He or she will make sure documents and contracts protect your interests and meet your needs, as well as the other parties'.

ONLINE BUSINESS

While online business is not an alternative business, it is a type that stands alone and that deserves to be introduced early in this book. There are references in the marketing chapter about how to use the Internet to get the word out and keep in touch with your customers; this section is specifically about creating an entirely cyberspace business, including marketing, sales, and payments. Online businesses are often home-based, and since so many people have home computers or computer access, it's easy for them to shop, trade, and find information and services online. It's easy to create a virtual enterprise.

Some advantages of selling on the Internet:

- A virtual store can be less expensive than bricks and mortar.
- The business is open to customers 24/7.
- Inventory management is easier, since there is no need for display.
- Potential markets are greater, nationally and internationally.
- The user-friendly website format can be convenient and accessible.

Some disadvantages of selling on the Internet:

- Customers cannot physically handle and inspect the merchandise.
- There may be more returns, particularly because customers cannot try on clothing before buying.

- There is no customer personal interface to help generate sales.
- It's an overcrowded marketplace; since it's relatively easy, everybody is doing it.
- Reliance on shipping to get merchandise to customers increases the likelihood of mishaps.

Starting with a home-based online enterprise may be a great way to test a business before making a major investment in renting space. Some products and services are especially conducive to Internet sales. For example:

- Anything that you can create and manufacture that is easy to ship, such as handicrafts or art
- Anything that can be purchased wholesale, such as books, collectibles, clothing, or software
- Financial, legal, writing, secretarial, design, and other services

Setting Up Your Website

The basic needs for a website are information about the product or service, about how to do business with you, and about payment arrangements. To get started, you will need a computer, a modem, an Internet connection, software, and an agreement with a company that will connect you to the Internet. A Web host is a company that leases you disk space for your website to sit on the Internet. An Internet service provider, or ISP, connects you to networks; among the providers are America Online (AOL), Microsoft Network (MSN), and EarthLink. For business, you will want high-speed Internet access such as DSL, which means you can transfer information from ten to fifty times faster than if you used a standard modem. Shop around for a Web host; check out prices; ask friends, family, and anyone you know who has a website for recommendations, since there are many, many options. You'll also need to be able to collect statistics so you can determine how many people visit your site, where they go after they leave, and other pertinent information.

Next you need to create a domain name, which identifies your business. Your uniform resource locator (URL), or website address, will be used by people who want to view your website and find your business. You want to be remembered easily, and you might want to indicate the type of business, but don't make the URL overly long and explanatory—no one wants to type forever. Most domain names end with ".com." Check to determine the availability of the name you select by going to the Whois feature at www.internic.net. You can also ask your provider to check for availability before your registration is complete.

Creating the Site

Your website is your face to the world, the representation of your business. It contains information and, typically, photos and links. You can do it yourself if you have some skills; they can be enhanced with content-creation software. If you don't do it yourself, get someone with experience in design and graphics to help you. You want the most attractive package to sell your product or service, and maximum ease of use for your site. Check out websites that appeal to you, and those of your competition. Your site can be simple, with one page of information, or more complex, with multiple pages where customers can learn more about who you are and examine your credentials for making a product or delivering a service. If you want to use pictures and you are not a photographer, avail yourself of a professional; there is nothing worse than tacky photos. And if you plan on updating your site or adding products or content in the future, make sure you have a format that allows for easy alterations and changes.

Once someone clicks on your site and has decided to buy, you have to provide a way for people to pay. Where is the cash register? The shopping cart has to make the payment process understandable, quick, easy, and safe. The customer must be able to make multiple purchases and browse back and forth between the shopping cart and other pages of your site; it should also be easy for customers to shop around. The most widely used payment service is PayPal; it has perfected itself to integrate seamlessly into many websites. PayPal automatically provides e-mail purchase receipts and gives you access to all transaction information, and there are no set-up costs; it also has its own credit card processor, and takes a transaction fee for each sale.

You will need to state your return and exchange policy on your website, so that customers know what to do if they are not satisfied with the merchandise or if they receive it damaged.

Product

The amount of product and the storing of your inventory have to be calculated on the basis of your money, space, expected demand, and replacement turnaround time. Shipping and handling fees must be calculated in the cost of doing business. The United States Postal Service is often the least expensive method of delivery, but you might explore other shipping companies to compare costs and timely delivery.

. . .

Building a website is like building a house—you can build a cottage or a mansion. With a website, what you get depends on how much money you have and what you need. You may start with a basic site, and add bells and whistles. Decide how much you have to spend and what you actually need to get the job done to make the sale.

Various companies offer inexpensive options that allow you to try before you buy. Etsy.com is an already built site that sells handmade products and has no start-up costs; it takes a portion of the sales, however. Shopify.com provides more flexibility as far as the items you sell, and offers a template to personalize your presentation. It also offers an e-commerce package with design, marketing, and sales. If online commerce works for you, jump in and join the thousands of cyber-entrepreneurs.

EXERCISE 3 • Would your business be appropriate as an online enterprise? Why or why not?

If it would be, complete the first steps to setting up your website:

- Research and evaluate at least five comparable websites, including those of your competition, taking note of what is done well and what needs improvement.
- Create your domain name and check the URL for availability.

- Evaluate and compare at least three Internet service providers.
- Obtain estimated shipping costs from at least three providers.
- Develop content for your website.
- Identify costs for the website start-up, including URL and domain name registration, monthly hosting fee, and maintenance charges.

HOW MUCH DO YOU WANT FOR THAT?

After you've defined your product or service and assessed your industry, you need to *determine pricing. Clearly, how much you charge is a key factor in relation to the profitability of your business.* In considering the pricing, you'll have to put a dollar amount on all the costs of making, buying, and delivering the product or service. If you have a service, it may take very little outlay of money, but your time is valuable. Many new business owners have difficulty putting a price on their time and end up undervaluing their services and not charging enough. It is better to slightly overcharge since it's more difficult to raise rather than lower fees. Start by comparing the pricing of the same or similar products. The competition can give you a general idea so that when you've added up the material and labor costs, you'll know if you have priced yourself out of the market. Keep in mind when creating your product that the costs for your initial run may be higher, so you'll need to factor in subsequent runs. A good example is greeting cards. I knew of an entrepreneur who designed cards and wanted to base her price on the upfront costs of her first batch and charge ten dollars per card. Obviously the price point was much too high compared to the Hallmark-type competition. After she reviewed the figures, it was clear to her that she couldn't try to recover start-up costs from the sale of her initial run. I finally persuaded her to charge $4.95; she could still make money by selling more cards and could calculate the total costs of subsequent print runs over a two-year period.

Another type of pricing, called *demand pricing*, is based on scarcity. It's when there are more customers and fewer products, so there is justification for jacking up the price. Take, for example, concert tickets. The face value may be one thing, but if it's a sold-out show, people will be willing to pay a premium price. Same thing for coveted goods. When the Xbox was introduced, it flew off the shelves and sold out in hours. Then anyone who had to have one paid double the sticker price.

Finally, there is *value-added pricing*. The product or service is basically the same, but you bring something that makes the customer feel it's worth more. Sometimes it can just be the name or brand, like Q-tips versus plain old cotton swab, but whatever it is, the customer perceives the value or benefit as greater and will pay more. The bottom line is that you want to cover your costs and make money.

Che Riley had an entrepreneurial idea running in her family but had to learn how to package and price it in order to create a successful enterprise.

Fledgling entrepreneurs often struggle to clearly define their product or service, but for Che Riley the idea for Nature's Nuggets, her line of home fragrances, was literally right under her nose. As a child, she got that same evasive reaction whenever she asked why certain family members traveled around with those "good-smelling" rocks. She grew up trying to figure out what kind of side hustle her family was doing on the down low, and it was years later that she learned exactly what was going on with those rocks and the fragrances. The family guarded the secret of the Heavenly Scented Rocks the way KFC guards its secret recipe of herbs and spices. The aunt who developed the product lived in another state, and Che was never able to actually see how it was done. Meanwhile, Che spent time pursuing her own career. With trade school training, she worked as a computer instructor in a not-for-profit center for underserved women and attended community college. In 2006, she earned a B.A. in corporate communications from Baruch College.

Once she realized her educational dream and got her degree, she decided to launch a business that would enhance her family's aromatherapy products. Che experimented with various ways to perfect the product, which was basically a natural nonburning way to enjoy aroma, using porous stones or crystals that had been infused with essential oils and fragrance. The decorative rocks and crystals give off a fragrance much like incense candles, air fresheners, or potpourri, but without the need to burn wax or wood, and the process is very labor intensive. Che purchases the stones and crystals, and in her "laboratory" (a rented space about the size of a large kitchen) she washes, polishes, colors, and infuses them with oil. To get a good, well-scented batch takes about four to six months of soaking.

Che quit her job and launched her business with a total of $17,000 in savings and money from a silent partner. She currently operates as a sole proprietor but would eventually like to form an LLC (limited liability company) with actual participating partners. Her initial investment was used to buy a *car, equipment, and supplies to make the products, pay rent for a small work space, and pay a small salary. With a total of $2,000 a month for business and personal expenses, she has exhausted her savings. But when Che factors in one-time-only start-up costs and the inflated cost for her initial run, she feels confident that her business will soon show some positive cash flow. The product is packaged in two-, four-, eight-, and sixteen-ounce jars, which sell for six, eight, ten, and fifteen dollars, respectively. In order to break even, she needs to sell $140 worth of products a day. In one year Che can purchase two thousand pounds of untreated nuggets for $6,000, which takes six months for infusing the scent. If she sells all of the nuggets in the next six months, she has made a profit of $28,000 after a year and after subtracting $12,000 in expenses. This is with Che doing all of the labor and sales. While this may not seem like very much money, Che has learned to live on a bare-bones budget. With the economic downturn, there are no meals consumed outside of the home except in the homes of friends and family. There is no money for personal care or extra clothing. This is a willing sacrifice for her dream.*

Her customers are people who burn incense and candles and also those who can't burn them because of allergies or space restrictions. Che has identified her customers as working class who tend to be more price conscious and want a longer-lasting fragrance because it's more economical. She markets directly to consumers at street fairs, festivals, and other places where people make impulse purchases. She also does wholesale by offering products to retailers, churches, and prophets who use the aroma to "catch the spirits."

Che looks to expand her distribution to commercial outlets as a space freshener for bathrooms, salons, and sanitation trucks. That means more face time and Che personally knocking on doors since her passion is often what clinches the sale. She hopes to make $50,000 in the next year and will focus on branding and beautifying the package with color, labeling, and a logo, making the world smell better one sale at a time.

Che has shown her business savvy by taking a family side gig and working to improve the concept and turn it into a viable enterprise. She's extremely cost and quality conscious and knows how to keep her overhead low. Her prices reflect this consciousness, and she's done precise cost breakdowns and knows exactly where her profit margins are.

Determining costs can't be done with a snapshot approach but should be figured on a timeline. Through repetition of the process and the purchase of initial one-time-only items, your actual costs may be much lower over time, like the greeting card example.

If you're in a service industry, the opposite may be true. It's the initial output of your time and the fast delivery of a service and subsequent payment that would generate higher revenue. But then there's the additional time-consuming things that you need to factor in. For example, if you run a bed-and-breakfast, your nightly rate must reflect the countless hours spent, often on intangibles. If you don't put a value on your time, it can burn you out and bury your business. You'll need to account for the cleaning time and the preparation time of the units, plus serving breakfast. If you are an event planner, your out-of-pocket expenses, like flowers, linens, tables, chairs, space decorations, and food, plus all the things you do to ensure that the event goes off without a hitch, should be valued. You have to add on your time and expertise in pulling it all together and pulling it off. Do you charge by the event, by the hour, or both? Is there an initial consultation fee? Would you consider a flat basic fee with additions charged by the hour? As a personal trainer, do you charge one hundred dollars per hour or sixty dollars? At the second rate, it would take five clients to make the same money as with three of the big spenders, but you might be more likely to attract more people with the lower rate. And if you lost one of the five, it would be less of a blow to your bottom line than losing one at the higher rate. You'll need to determine how many clients it will take for you to break even and then make a profit. If you are home-based, your expenses are lower and you can charge less to be more competitive in the marketplace. And take a look at the competition to get a general idea about how to set your prices.

In the book business, there is an industry standard of 60/40. The books are purchased at a 40 percent discount or markup. A customer pays twenty dollars for a book that costs the bookseller twelve dollars, therefore a profit is made of eight dollars. The price is clearly marked on the book by the publisher. Discounting wasn't really an option because, based on my overall expenditures, if I cut prices, my margin would be too low and I wouldn't have turned a profit. This is in contrast to other retail products like jewelry or liquor, which may have a markup of 100 percent or more.

EXERCISE 3 • Complete this exercise so you'll know what you need to charge to cover your costs and whether you can realistically make a profit.

How much will you charge, and how did you determine the price?

How much money do you expect to generate?

How many units of your products or service do you need to sell to make that profit?

COVER YOUR ASS(ETS)

Just like a firewall and security system to protect your computer, you need to protect your idea. The most common ways to protect you are through:

- *Copyright:* A legal protection to the author of original works that are fixed in tangible forms of expression. It is most commonly used to prevent persons from reproducing, selling, or distributing literary, musical, and dramatic works without your permission. If you are an author, be sure to copyright your book.
- *Patent:* Granted by the government, it provides exclusive rights to make or sell an invention for a specific time. To be considered, your invention must be novel, unique, or new; useful by accomplishing something or serving some purpose; or not obvious, meaning a skilled person in a particular field of interest would view the invention as an unexpected or surprising development. So it has to do something significantly different.
- *Trademark:* A safeguard to prevent others from the use of words or symbols that are the same or like the ones you have created or selected to represent your business. This is usually your name and your logo. Both the name Hue-man Bookstore and its logo are trademarked.

EXERCISE 4 • Do you need to copyright, patent, or trademark, and if so, why? By determining this in the preliminary stages, you can sidestep potential legal problems regarding proprietary rights down the road.

Add this to the exercises from Chapter One, and you now have clearly defined your product or service and will have a good estimate of the price you'll charge.

Chapter Three

Step 3

Get the 411 on Who's Doing What, Where, and How: Research Your Competition

In 1984, when I opened my first bookstore in Denver, the only competition was the Tattered Cover, which at that time was the largest independent bookstore in the country. It had an African-American section with additional ethnic titles throughout the store. The Tattered Cover had a national reputation and was the primary source of books in the area. . . . it was like the Barnes & Noble of its day.

When I opened the second Hue-Man Bookstore in 2003, the industry landscape was vastly different. Now we were up against Amazon, the online bookselling giant, and other book superstores in all the major cities. I researched all the bookstores in Harlem and the surrounding areas, including the chains and independents. I also visited nonbookstores like Wal-Mart, Costco, Target, as well as grocery stores and drugstores. I went online to check out Amazon, even ordering books to get a feel for their customer service and how much time it actually took to ship books to my home. But I found my main competition was right outside my door. The street vendors were moving the merchandise. They had almost zero overhead and their "store" consisted of tables stacked with books. They carried a respectable selection, from chick lit to gritty urban fiction, as well as classics from Zora Neale Hurston to James Baldwin. And they were there to stay, protected by the first amendment.

Instead of being discouraged by all that competition, I found a way to use it to my advantage. My competitors provided a wealth of information and I studied each one to determine the numbers and demographics of their African-American customers. I looked at the types of books they sold and how much space they devoted to African-American titles. I attended book signings for African-American authors and spoke with the sales representatives and publicity staff that the publisher sent with the author. I was particularly interested in how many African-American authors they represented and how many books they sold at the events. I cozied up to the African-American staff and publishing staff, since they were willing to talk to me more openly and give me the "real deal."

This chapter will show you how to identify and evaluate your competition and determine how they impact your business and compete for your customer base. "Keep your friends close and your enemies closer," the saying goes, and it definitely holds true in business, since the more you know about your competition, the better equipped you'll be to deflect and manage them. Step 3 is also geared to get you to think about how you will differentiate yourself from other similar businesses and position your enterprise to stand out in an often overcrowded marketplace.

. . .

So you think you have this great idea and that your business will be unique and totally different. Brace yourself. *It's probably not.* You might be as creative and innovative as you want to be, but the bad news is that someone else has probably already been there and done that. That doesn't mean you can't capitalize on their business idea. The good news is there's almost always room for expansion in the marketplace, and you don't need to reinvent the wheel to be successful. Just reinterpret it and start by using your existing competition as a resource tool. There will be competition in almost every industry, so use what's already out there and then organize your search to make the best use of your time, energy, and money. In this chapter we will work to answer the following questions about your competitors:

Who is your competition?

What do you want to know about your competition?

How can you get information about your competition?

Your primary competitors are most likely businesses that are within walking distance in your neighborhood and those within a five-to-ten-mile radius. A quick way to find them is by searching the Internet and business directory using a zip code.

There are three basic types of competition.

1. *Direct competitors.* People who are doing what you want to do, selling the same or very similar products and services to your potential or current customers. These are the ones who have been

around for a while and will be in your face and go head-to-head with you for clientele.

2. *Indirect.* People who are selling the same product or provide a similar service, but it's not the only product or service that they sell. They most likely have other sources of revenue, but they still sell enough of your product to seriously hurt your sales. A good example is if you run a bakery. Then your indirect competition is the corner café or coffee shop that sells baked goods.

3. *New business.* The last type is a business that springs up after you've opened and jumps into your mix. It might be a former customer or someone who's tracked your success and then decides to open a similar business in your own backyard.

Once you've identified your competition, you'll need to find out everything you can about them. The first and easiest way to learn about who else is playing in your sandbox is through their advertisements and what they say about themselves. To let people know who they are, all businesses have some type of literature, like business cards, brochures, flyers, press releases, and listings in the Yellow Pages. Note the types of ads they place, and whether they are basic or display, with graphics and photos. Look the companies up online to see if and how they use the Internet. Check out their websites for content, presentation, and the professional quality of their ads. Do they promote their websites and use e-mail addresses? While you are looking at content, you also want to see how they are presenting themselves and if they have a hook or some unique characteristic relating to the business or the owners. Do they advertise with incentives? Do they participate in the trade associations and have developed partnerships and affiliations?

Jai Jai Greenfield opened Harlem Vintage, but not before making a thorough evaluation of the competition and doing lots of research on the front end to pave the path for success on the back end.

Entrepreneurs Jai Jai Greenfield and Eric Woods saw trendy Harlem as ripe with wine enthusiasts ready to be plucked. At the time, the only place in the neighborhood to buy wine was the liquor and lotto stores that sold cheap wine and mini-bottles from behind a bulletproof glass. There was no place for people to get their higher-end drink, and that lack of competition and upscale customer base made it a perfect place for their boutique wine store. Jai Jai, no stranger to targeted sales and marketing research, developed her aptitude for customer relations with the big boys on Wall Street. She climbed the corporate ladder for nearly a decade working at Smith Barney, Goldman Sachs, and finally Morgan Stanley in the firm's sales and trading division. She is outgoing, articulate, bright, bubbly, and with high energy (what would later be an apt description of some of her wines). Her multitasking and sales experiences served her well in the corporate world and were significant assets when connecting with customers as an entrepreneur. Client entertainment, a big part of her former job, taught her people skills, and as a result of many client dinners, she developed an appreciation for wine and became a true oenophile. She studied everything from the grape to the cork, and was certified by the Wine & Spirit Education Trust.

The store, Harlem Vintage, was born out of a discussion with a long-time friend about the lack of shops in the neighborhood dedicated to selling just wine. That inspired their vision, to create a wine experience where customers could browse, taste, socialize, and learn about wine. Jai Jai and Eric formed a partnership, and a corporation for liability purposes, and began to research the feasibility of their concept. They distributed more than five hundred questionnaires at community events to get feedback. Just by talking to people, they learned who their potential buyers were, how much they spent on wine, and where they shopped. The partners also went to local liquor stores to determine the shelf space devoted to wine, what kind, and how much was sold. Zoning was another issue, since stores that sold alcohol were restricted by distance from churches and schools. After they evaluated all of their research, their verdict was favorable. There was a sustainable market and a population that would support an upscale wine experience uptown. They specifically sought out a Harlem female designer to create the beautifully designed store, which opened its doors in 2004. Coincidentally, on the same day of their opening, another wine store opened a mile away. Two years later, a former customer opened up four blocks away, so now there are two wine stores within a half-mile if each other. When Jai Jai and Eric conceived their idea, they had competition in mind. They knew they had to make their store stand apart from the crowd, since it would be only a matter of time before someone else would see the fertile ground. They put a unique spin on their store layout, arranging wines by type, grape, and characteristic instead of by region, and featured products from people of color. This created a user-friendly environment to enhance wine knowledge and encourage conversation.

So far Jai Jai and Eric are on target for sales projections. Although the challenge is market penetration (i.e., reaching their customer), the wine tastings and sponsorship of community events have generated an excellent customer base, and Jai Jai and Eric are on track to make the first million in sales. Another way of defusing the increased competition was to create a wine bar in the adjoining space that has added a new dimension to create an additional destination.

Jai Jai and Eric were careful not to let their enthusiasm about their business cloud their good judgment. Instead of blindly leaping in, they conducted feasibility studies and surveys before deciding it would be profitable to move forward. And they also had a specific strategy to create an experience that was unique in the area, and they initially had no real direct competition.

EXERCISE 1 • By completing this exercise, you'll get the 411 on who's out there, what they're doing, and how well they're doing it.

List all of your competitors and everything you've found out about them from your research, including who they are, what they're selling, where they're located, and how much they charge.

Keep a folder of all your information about your competition, especially those who are your direct competitors.

Finding out about the competition is a critical part of your business research, but some of the best information is gathered from just paying attention and listening to what people have to say about the other vendors in your marketplace. First, you need to *discover the word out on the street:* it's the fastest, easiest, and cheapest way to find out about your competition. You'll want to get an idea about how your competition presents itself and what others are saying, so ask around. It's a simple way to research your competition, and it also gives you a measure of how effective they are at getting the word out about their business.

- *Pay close attention to the views of customers and the value they place on the service or product you're offering.* Customers are the ultimate source to get the lowdown on the competition. Ask people where they are currently buying the same goods or services you intend to sell, and they'll give you a wealth of information. People love to talk. Think of the last time you complimented your label-loving neighbor on her "to die for" Escada ensemble and she gave you the whole backstory of the hidden-away designer boutique with the best prices and *fine* store manager.
- *Look for articles written about the competition.* Even those generated from their own press releases or in response to their public relations campaign, although they might be biased, still show how a business has worked to make itself newsworthy.
- *Check out directories.* They're easily accessed sources of information. These guidebooks are produced by associations to promote their members and typically give a brief description of the business and their products and services. You should make it a point to put in some face time at association events.
- *Attend a trade association meeting.* Put on your power pantsuit and talk firsthand to people in your industry. It will give you a chance to pick the brains of experts and learn the all-important skill of social networking. Remember, it's not just what you know but also who you know.
- *Talk to vendors and suppliers.* Be nosy, channel your favorite CSI character, and ask lots of questions to get a sense of how the competition does business. Find out if they're on credit hold

and if they must prepay vendors or pay COD because they're no longer extended credit. This indicates a poor payment history and is a big red flag signaling that a business is in trouble.

- *Pay your competition a "social call."* You can find out a lot about a business by visiting and observing what they're doing. Pay attention to the employees and watch how they provide customer service. And don't be cheap; buy something. If you're thinking of opening a salon, schedule an appointment for a spa service, for "research," and take note of the entire interaction, from confirming the appointment to how you're greeted and then finally how you're addressed as you leave. Evaluate the premises. Do you find them neat and inviting, or disorderly and chaotic? Start up conversations with the owners and salespeople by passing out generous compliments, which always gets a positive response and will open up the gates for bragging rights to come through. If possible, consider working or volunteering in the business in order to get firsthand information.

- *After you've done all your legwork, use your computer to gather information online.* Internet searches on Google or Yahoo! will produce a huge stream of data, including critiques and ratings, particularly if you're in the food industry. The Internet also has the most current statistics and provides up-to-the-minute news. Another place to do your research is the library's business section, which can provide historical information and background about your industry. Don't forget media outlets like your local newspaper, magazines, radio, and TV stations. Local, state, and federal government agencies like the Office of Small Business Development Centers also carry information about businesses.

When evaluating the competition, here's what to look for:

1. *Name and logo.* How do they convey the message of the business and how are they visually represented?
2. *Products and services offered.* Look at the complete range, plus the customer service. How is the presentation and packaging? Is any particular merchandise moving better than other items?
3. *Pricing policy.* Consider the price based on the quality and discounts. Are there any additional benefits that the customers can perceive if the pricing is higher than industry norms?
4. *Customers.* Who are they, and what can you tell about them from your observation? What are they buying and in what quantities?
5. *Promotion.* What are they doing to promote themselves and attract customers, and how is it working?
6. *Suppliers and vendors.* Where do they get what they sell? If it is a service, what are their credentials and experience?
7. *Position in the industry.* How much business do they capture, and can you determine their market share and segment?
8. *Financials.* Are they secure? This may be difficult to pinpoint, but you can get some sense from the traffic when the cash register is getting a workout. Depending on your detective skills, you can ask key people who know about the business.
9. *Organizational structure.* How have they put together their business, the workforce, work space, and operations?
10. *Strengths and weaknesses.* What is it that they are doing well, and what isn't working?

Anne-Kerr Kennedy started her yoga clothing business based on what she perceived as a need and worked to create a product to fill that niche.

In 1998, a running injury brought Anne-Kerr (A.K.) to her first yoga class. What she found was not only relief for her physical pain but also a sense of emotional well-being. In no time, she was hooked, taking classes three to four times a week. She was devoted to her practice and loved the classes and the entire yoga experience, but the clothes, not so much. For A.K., making a mind/body connection and being relaxed mentally and physically was integral to her yoga, so wearing comfortable clothing was a key component. But the majority of the clothes she found were made from synthetic materials, were restrictive, and didn't breathe. She and her friends had difficulty finding durable, natural, comfortable yoga clothes that were still stylish and fit well. Opportunity came calling or perhaps chanting. A.K. recognized this unfilled niche and started to explore the idea of bringing something new to the market by designing and manufacturing yoga clothing made from natural breathable fabrics. And in 2005, A.K. launched Hyde Yoga; her mission, to create a clothing line as purposeful and practical as yoga.

A.K.'s competition in the yoga clothing business is generally two types, indirect competitors, those that sell sporting goods and yoga clothes, and direct competitors, those who sell yoga clothes exclusively. Nike the thousand-pound gorilla is a major indirect competitor. It sells shoes, active sportswear, and every other sports- and exercise-related thing on the planet, but the majority of its clothing is made from synthetic fabrics. A more direct competitor is Patagonia, a climbing apparel company that sells synthetic and organic cotton yoga clothing. A.K.'s most direct competitor is Lulu Lemon, which does $150 million in annual sales and carries a wide variety of sporty synthetic and natural-fiber yoga clothing, which is its primary business. Add to that the bunches of what A.K. calls "hippie dippies," the very small local companies that make clothing but don't really represent serious competition. In order for A.K. to manage competition, she keeps a sharp eye on her bottom line, and the pricing of her product does not exceed more than 50 percent of costs.

A.K. started out with a degree in English literature, but after graduation got a job designing trail maps and brochures in Aspen, Colorado. This began a process of developing her creative artistic side, which resulted in a master's degree in the College of Arts in Los Angeles. She worked for four years in a small rug design company that allowed her to develop business skills and prepare for the entrepreneurial leap. She developed her business plan while working the day job and started Hyde Yoga with $50,000 in savings.

Hyde Yoga started out as a home-based company; she used her parents' basement as a warehouse and has expanded and now rents a small space to house herself and two part-time employees who handle sales. She has a website that generates only 10 percent of retail sales, with the balance coming *from wholesale to yoga studios and retail outlets across the country. Initially a one-person operation with twenty orders, she generated sales of $200,000 and is on target for a second year of $700,000 in revenues. The goal for Hyde is to increase revenues by upgrading the website and hiring salespeople to hit the road to expand their market. The sales force will also provide her relief from the day-to-day management so A.K. can concentrate on business development. She is savvy and aggressive and will easily build her business beyond a million-dollar operation.*

"Graceful Gear" is A.K.'s slogan, and it's also the way she differentiates herself from her competition. In an arguably oversaturated exercise apparel market, she remains focused on yoga clothes and has taken it a step further by using only organic, breathable fabrics. By creating a specialty product, Anne has been able to attract a specific but sizable customer base.

Now that you have collected information, what do you do with it? You can assess your competitors' performance against what you are doing and planning to do. Then replicate the strengths and exploit the weaknesses and work to improve on their ideas in order to take your business to the next level. Having an awareness and even an appreciation of how your competitors serve their customers and suppliers can help you keep your business focused and on target. You may even find ways to join with the competition to develop a strategy against a common foe. Competition also keeps you from becoming complacent, since feeling that hot breath on the back of your neck can be a great motivator. It's what keeps the juices flowing in order to stay ahead and on top of the game.

> **EXERCISE 3** • Now it's time to judge yourself and measure how you stack up.
>
> On the basis of the information you gathered, and judging from how you evaluated your top three competitors, how would you rate your business and what you do?
>
> List what you plan to do better or differently to stand out.

Not only does learning about the competition show you who you'll be in the ring with, but it will also help you sidestep obstacles and save you time and money by avoiding their mistakes. Information about competitors also teaches you about your industry, and the following chapters will help you by providing real-world examples, good or bad, of how others do business.

Chapter Four

Step 4 Create Your Launching Pad: Determine Your Business Form and Structure

When it was time for me to decide on the structure of the bookstore, I relied on the expertise of our attorney. He suggested a Subchapter S Corporation, which at the time made as much sense to me as a flea-flicker quarterback reverse. I was basically clueless about the distinctions among the types of business structures. Fortunately, the attorney knew the right questions to ask. We talked about the vision for the business, and our attorney developed the initial organization, mapping out a long-term strategy to plan ahead for possible changes in ownership and the addition of shareholders. We began as a three-person operation, with two shareholders and one employee, and the attorney questioned us extensively about the partners' relationship, vision, and responsibilities. We anticipated that the business would not make money in the beginning, so we would use the losses individually as tax write-offs. We also prepared for the addition of shareholders, and a Subchapter S Corporation would allow us to do just that. In the beginning, we had to use our own money to meet all of our funding needs, since before we opened our doors, we were just another unknown start-up and no one was willing to invest in the business.

A good attorney will examine worst-case scenarios and plan accordingly. Luckily, we were blessed with one who attended to details, since within eighteen months one of the owners wanted out. Because of the agreement, the departure occurred in an orderly fashion and did not disrupt the business. Once we were up and running, we were able to attract a group of very loyal customers, some of whom became shareholders and wanted to support their community bookstore. This allowed us to raise capital to purchase our building. As we became more successful, we shifted from an S Corporation to a C Corporation.

Get ready for the legalese. This chapter takes you step-by-step through the process of determining your business structure. It will give you an understandable but comprehensive explanation of each form, as well as suggestions on what business type is better suited for each one.

As you get ready to formalize your business structure, you'll need to address your wants and needs and balance them with *reality*. When you are selecting the form of your enterprise, the issue of ownership is probably the first thing to resolve. For example, total ownership might sound great and allow you to unleash your inner diva control freak, but operating in the real world might mean that you need to include other people to share your proprietorship and decision making. Among the factors to consider are initial financial contributions, the possibility of partners, their roles, your current financial status, and even your marital status.

If you decide to start your business with others, consider your relationship with them. People frequently recruit family members as part-ners, but before you set up shop with relatives, get a reality check about your own family dynamics. Is your family like the Huxtables or more like the Sopranos? Determine if you have any long-standing issues or grievances that need to be resolved before moving forward. Then decide on the details of the association. Will they contribute financially? What will the agreement be about the money? Will it be an investment, loan, or salary? How much of the business are you willing to relinquish for an investment? Who will be the operating manager making the day-to-day decisions and who will be entitled to a salary? If they loan you money, what are the interest rate and the payback arrangement?

As your entrepreneurial venture begins to take shape, you'll recognize that being self-employed does not mean doing it all by yourself. Success depends on a support team of specialized professionals who will enhance the business. Think of them as your quartet of superheroes, each with unique powers to serve your enterprise.

YOUR FIRST SUPERHERO

Enter the *attorney*, your first superhero. In order to move forward and formal-ize your enterprise, you will need an attorney, able to leap over mountains of paperwork and cut through red tape in a single bound. Well, not quite, but they will help you decipher lawyer-speak and assist in the decision about the form of your business. An attorney will formalize the rules of partnerships and shareholders and anticipate what to do if things go wrong. Your lawyer will also complete the necessary paperwork for registration of your business and review the contracts necessary when working with contractors.

Before you retain an attorney, do some homework to help you better understand what type of corporate structure best serves your needs. Prior to scheduling a meeting, learn about the various business structures by doing research online, at libraries, or at bookstores. By doing your own legwork, you'll save time, which translates into saving money when meeting with a bill-by-the-hour professional. The attorney will familiarize you with the various business models, their general characteristics, tax consequences, and the advantages and disadvantages of each. Then they will find the structure that works best for your enterprise.

Review the attached grid for an overview of business structures:

TYPE	DESCRIPTION	LIABILITY	TAX CONSEQUENCES	ADVANTAGES	DISADVANTAGES
Sole Proprietorship	One owner who maintains complete control.	All obligations of the business rest with the owner. In the event of a lawsuit, the owner's personal assets can be accessed.	Considered a "nontaxable" entity, business assets and liabilities are not separate from owner who files all income and expenses on her personal income tax return.	Easiest and cheapest legal business form to start and requires much less paperwork.	Owner is totally liable for all business and risks personal assets. Business ends with the owner's death or departure.
General Partnership	Has two or more persons who share the management responsibilities, profits and losses of the business.	Each partner is responsible for all business liabilities including debts and taxes.	Each partner reports business income and expenses on individual tax returns. Legally the business is not viewed as a separated taxable entity.	Relatively inexpensive and easy to start and operate.	Unless a partnership agreement is put in place, their partnership ends with the death or withdrawal of one of the partners. All partners are held liable for all business debts, risking personal assets.

TYPE	DESCRIPTION	LIABILITY	TAX CONSEQUENCES	ADVANTAGES	DISADVANTAGES
Limited Partnership	Has two classes of partners, general and limited partners, with the general partner in control of the business.	General partners are held responsible for all business obligations. Limited partners are only liable for proportionally the amount they've invested in the business.	Both general and limited partners report business income and expenses on individual tax returns.	Limited partners' liability for business debts is limited to their investment as long as they do not engage in the daily operations of the business.	General partners are held liable for all business debts. Partnership could end with the death or withdrawal of a general partner when a partnership is not in place.
Corporation	Owned by shareholders. Structure includes a board of directors and corporate officers.	Limits personal liability of shareholders.	Considered a separate and distinct business entity, a corporation pays its own taxes. Shareholders pay taxes on their individual dividends.	Shareholders have limited liability for business debts. A corporation has a perpetual life since it can survive the deaths or withdrawals of shareholders.	More expensive and complex to start than a partnership or sole proprietorship. A separate taxable entity subject to both state and federal taxes.
Subchapter S Corporation	Has no more than 75 shareholders. Includes a board of directors and corporate officers.	Shareholders are responsible for the amount of their investment.	Each shareholder pays taxes and reports business profits and losses on individual returns.	Shareholders have limited personal liability. Does not suffer from double taxation. Can survive the deaths or withdrawals of shareholders, owners, and partners.	All shareholders' profits and losses are allocated based on the number of stock shares. More expensive to launch. Limited number of owners, all of whom must agree to file under this type of form.

TYPE	DESCRIPTION	LIABILITY	TAX CONSEQUENCES	ADVANTAGES	DISADVANTAGES
Limited Liability Company	Has two or more members, who all have authority within the business.	Members are not responsible for business debts.	Partners' income and expenses are reported on individual tax returns.	Members can participate in daily activities of business and still sustain their limited liability status. Profit or loss is not distributed according to stock shares.	Rules governing limited liability companies differ according to the state. Generally, the consent of members is needed before transferring the business.

Donna Vassallo is an example of a sole proprietorship. Her story demonstrates how she selected her business form based on the type of organization while also taking into account future projections.

Donna's business is called MarketingWorks NY—and that's exactly what she does, work. She writes and edits copy for brochures, websites, and sell sheets, and does competitive research for firms designing marketing and advertising materials, and as a sole proprietor, she does it all herself. By incorporating as a sole proprietorship she represents one of the most common business forms. For Donna it was the best option, since her business required little upfront capital and is home-based in a separate space in her co-op apartment. She is the only person working and has complete control of the business. With a sole proprietorship, she could start her business with minimal cost and paperwork, and although liability rests with the owner, Donna's exposure to risk is limited. With a sole proprietorship, she can still separate her personal finances and not commingle with business funds.

Donna's journey started in Boston, where she moved after receiving a degree in history from Holy Cross College. She started out as a secretary for an advertising agency and worked her way up to account manager, a position in which she learned to be detail-oriented, an analytical thinker, and a problem solver. Wanting to expand her business skills, she decided to take a course called Effective Written Communication as part of Harvard's business administration program, and it was there that she discovered her passion. The professor told her that she had a talent for writing, something that she'd never recognized. Prompted by those encouraging words and the fact that her ad agency job was rather dissatisfying, she quit her job and traveled internationally for four years, and along the way she got paid for writing travel articles with her own byline. She eventually came to New York and settled at a travel agency, where she started writing proposals. Over time, she racked up more experience by developing newsletters and other marketing materials. When American Express purchased the travel agency, Donna decided it was time to cut the corporate apron strings, and left to try her hand as a freelancer. She took with her a severance package, savings, unemployment insurance, and stayed busy with several writing projects from American Express. But after 9/11, American Express reduced outsourcing and the contract work dwindled. Fortunately, Donna found work from a former coworker who owned a design firm and needed an outsourced writer for marketing materials. This relationship proved to be an inspiration, and in 2002, Donna launched writing as a real business. She learned from friends and colleagues about managing her fledgling enterprise and joined the local chapter of the National Association of Women Business Owners (NAWBO), a dues-based organization that represents the interests of women entrepreneurs, with nearly eighty chapters nationwide. It offers facilitated networking, educational programs, inspirational speakers, and special events to help members grow their business. Donna was actively involved in the communication committee and eventually became an officer. Her participation in NAWBO created visibility for her company and became a feeder for referrals.

Donna has two main sources for clients. One is her original coworker, whose firm has grown significantly and represents 40 percent of her business. The other source, another graphic designer, whom Donna met through NAWBO, owns two design firms that specialize in the high-performance computing industry. Donna gets the remainder of her work through networking and repeat business. Over the years, she has learned to streamline her billing process using a spreadsheet which showed that she needed to raise her rates. She learned the hard way that she wasn't charging enough and that she needed to have a more systematic approach to pricing. Donna now lists each project and the work required, such as creating brochures, sell sheets, websites, or advertising. She estimates the size of the job, amount of editorial content, the number of pages, and how long it will take to generate them. She then multiplies the total by an hourly rate. To that figure, she adds on charges for product development, service delivery, research, editing, and meetings. Although she's a one-woman show, Donna has become extremely efficient at managing her business and works a straight forty-hour week. Although Donna's revenues are under six figures, she is a single woman with a frugal lifestyle, who owns her co-op apartment, which has significantly appreciated in value. With her home-based business, she has the freedom to do the work she enjoys and indulge her passion for travel.

Donna's business is basically, well, just Donna. She's home-based and has no employees and essentially does everything herself. Any plans for expansion are fairly modest, so organizing as a sole proprietorship was the best option. It's fairly simple to execute and not overly complicated but still offers a degree of protection and the ability to separate business from personal funds.

. . .

Below you'll learn about the pros and cons of each type of business structure and who typically uses each kind:

SOLE PROPRIETORSHIP: The most common form and represents a majority of small businesses in the United States. People who are just starting out often choose this until it's practical to enter into a partnership or incorporate.

Pros: Ease and flexibility. Although perceived as small because it has only one owner, there are no restrictions on the size of the business or number of employees. You can register in the state or county by filing under your own name with your social security number, or select a "fictitious name" DBA (doing business as) to appear more professional. You can also apply for a Federal Tax ID Number.

Cons: Everything rests on your shoulders, and if there is any financial liability, it all comes back to you, so your personal assets are at risk. If you are sued for a breach of contract or there are outstanding debts, the claimant can take your money and your house. Since this business has to be limited to one individual, there is no opportunity to bring in other people.

PARTNERSHIP: Made up of individuals who want an equal or predetermined stake in the business.

Pros: Shared resources, decision making, and financial responsibilities. A partnership also helps prevent "brain drain" by giving you someone with whom you can strategize.

Cons: It requires more paperwork, since it's important to include terms relating to the distribution of the profits and each partner's rights, liabilities, and responsibilities within the written agreement. A partnership is also risky because of the fragility of relationships and the difficulty in buying out a partner.

LIMITED PARTNERSHIP: Frequently used by husband-and-wife teams. Often it starts out as the wife's enterprise, and later they decide to include the husband as a partner, although the wife remains the general partner. This is just another type of partnership but with two classes of partners, with the general partner having considerably more responsibility and control over the day-to-day operations.

Pros: It's an easy arrangement, and it offers a way for other people who believe in and trust the judgment of the general partner to invest in the company.

Cons: The inequality can also cause conflict.

C CORPORATION: An organizational structure that can sell stock to raise capital for the business. Authority to delegate the day-to-day operations is given to the board of directors and company officers who hire an employee usually titled executive director. This can be used by a business that is organized under another structure, like an S Corporation, and has begun to break even, make a profit, or wants to add other people. The corporation is a separate entity and has at least one meeting a year of directors and shareholders that includes an election of the directors. A C Corporation has officers, records minutes, and issues stock certificates. There is no limit to the number of shareholders. It is important that you hire an attorney to put together your business form and get counsel on adherence to the rules, since not fulfilling the formalities may jeopardize the veil of protection a corporation provides from personal liability.

Pros: This form protects personal assets and is excellent for persons with deep pockets who need to have their money shielded.

Cons: It's complex. The paperwork filed with the Secretary of State must include Articles of Incorporation and Bylaws that state the powers, limitation, and constitution for governing the corporation.

S CORPORATION: The corporate form of business structure that is heavily regulated because of the complicated tax implications and certain criteria that must be satisfied to qualify in accordance with the state where the business is incorporated. This form works best when the business has losses that can be applied against the owners' personal income for a tax advantage. It has all the characteristics and structure of a C Corporation; however, it is limited to no more than seventy-five shareholders.

Pros: Business gains and losses are passed through to the owners (shareholders). Regardless of your income status, you want to take the losses to reduce your taxes.

Cons: You must carefully plan with an accountant to avoid a huge personal tax bill at the end of a successful year because the business revenue will be reported on your personal income statement.

LIMITED LIABILITY COMPANY (LLC): A hybrid type of legal entity with qualities of both a corporation and a partnership. It is called a company and has members instead of shareholders. For federal tax purposes an LLC is usually treated like a general partnership.

The member's assets are protected against the company liability, but the income and losses generated by the business are passed through to the individual members and any income is taxed according to the member's personal tax rate.

Pros: It has more fluidity with respect to the member types. You may have an unlimited number of members who can own different classes of stocks. Members can be involved in the management of the business without losing their liability protection status and the business is not dissolved with the withdrawal of members.

Cons: There is a restriction on transferability of interest. One member of the company cannot transfer their interest or stock without the permission or consent of the other members. This structure requires explicit set-up rules, since it's a new type of form, and has no unified set of tax laws, except those created by individual states. Therefore, it is critical to check with state regulations.

PROFESSIONAL CORPORATION: A form of business for professional licensed-service-provider entrepreneurs, including doctors, lawyers, dentists, accountants, and psychologists, who then use PC after their name or the company name. The professional is the only shareholder.

Pros: Very easy to set up and the corporation shields personal assets.

Cons: It does not offer protection from malpractice awards.

At a glance, certain business structures sound appealing, but you'd better check your ego and take a hard look at what form would best suit the current and anticipated needs of your business. General considerations for choosing a particular legal structure should be based on the amount of risk you're willing to assume, owners' potential liability, continuity of the business, access to capital, management skills, and the purpose for starting the business.

EXERCISE 1 • According to your situation, determine which is the best form for you, and why. When answering this question, take into account the size of your enterprise and whether you will need partners in the beginning or plan to add them in the future. Also consider liability matters related to your business, the type of protection you will need, and how much personal risk you are willing to assume.

Maria Dowd shows the various business forms and how she had to change structures based on her business transitions.

When Maria launched Soul Journeys, in San Diego, she craved independence and autonomy, so she set up as a sole proprietorship. Later she had a reality check about the pitfalls of going it alone. Before becoming an entrepreneur, Maria was on a more traditional career path. She attended college and earned a degree in public administration at Cal State. Maria then settled into a comfortable routine as a married mother of two, working in sales and marketing for a shopping center promotions company. It was then that she had her "aha" moment and considered going into business for herself. She weighed the pros and cons and thought that as an entrepreneur she would have more choices, more freedom, and a better quality of life, so she struck out on her own. Her first client was Essence *magazine. At her previous job she had worked with the publication to create events at the shopping center to promote and showcase the magazine and generate exposure for* Essence *and its advertisers. In her new business* Essence *hired her to stage events at local venues, which evolved into developing empowerment conferences in major U.S. cities. The conferences gained traction and over a thirteen-year period African American Women on Tour touched the lives of more than twenty thousand women and girls, using powerful words to inform, inspire, and motivate.*

Maria started her business as a sole proprietor since she was essentially a one-woman operation with one client. Her accountant suggested an S Corporation to shield her assets and take advantage of the business losses for tax purposes. Like most start-ups, the business racked up losses that Maria could apply when filing her taxes in order to reduce her tax liability. Although a corporation on paper, Maria did not put in place a structure and functioned much like a sole proprietor. By keeping it contained as an S Corporation, Maria thought she could better control her enterprise, but without people around her with business savvy, she made emotional decisions that were not in the best interest of the business. Her expenses were not in line with the revenue stream, and she was never able to create a sustainable business model. In 2003, she was so deep in the red that she had to shut down the business. With a daughter at home and a mountain of debt, she had to do something. Her lifeboat came in the form of one of her former vendors, Warm Spirit, a direct-selling company that had been a sponsor of African American Women on Tour. For only a hundred dollars, she learned, she could become a rep for a line of botanical skin care products. She figured that with her existing networking, sales, and marketing skills, she could build a sales force of recruits to increase her compensation and make her investment work.

Working with Warm Spirit was a great opportunity and gave Maria the flexibility and leverage to expand her entrepreneurial endeavors. She could still maintain the S Corporation. For Maria, making the switch to direct selling was the right call. She's involved with a national brand with a support system, and the money has been good. After seven years, her income grew substantially, and she expected to reach a compensation level to support a comfortable and satisfying lifestyle when Warm Spirit went out of business.

Incorporating her skills as a public speaker and author and leveraging the relationships and goodwill created from African American Women on Tour and Warm Spirit, Maria has taken direct selling up a notch. She was recently named the exclusive San Diego distributor for Design Essentials professional hair-care products and has formed a sole proprietorship for the new business, selling the products to salons, hair stylists, and cosmetology schools. She is on track not only to survive but to thrive as well.

Maria's story demonstrates the importance of working closely with an attorney to help select the proper form for the specific stage your business is in. By prematurely organizing as a sole proprietorship, she suffered losses and eventually had to start over with a different venture and a different structure. The second time around, she let the business dictate the form and has been able to better manage her resources by using a Subchapter S. With the new business she has added another form and demonstrated how to take advantage of having multiple business structures when doing a variety of projects.

EXERCISE 2 • If you plan to have partners, who will be the principals or managing partner?

What will each partner contribute, and what will each partner's percentage and ownership be?

What will be the partner's roles and responsibilities?

Choosing a form is complex and critical. Once you've determined your business type, add that to your work in the previous chapters. Now your idea is becoming a real flesh-and-bones entity, with structure and substance.

Chapter Five

Step 5

Ka-ching! Show Me the Money: How Much Will It Take, and Where Will You Get It?

For the first Hue-Man Bookstore, I didn't even bother to go to a bank. As a former banker, I knew that if I were my client, I wouldn't have loaned me money. I had no competence or experience in the book business, no collateral except for my substantial retirement fund, which I was not willing to risk, and no sure way to service the debt. My only guarantee was an earnest promise to myself that I would make money. As it turned out, I was overconfident and underqualified and wouldn't have been able to repay a loan. Even though I was devoted to the business full-time, money was tight in the beginning, and I didn't even have enough to pay myself a salary. I was also under the mistaken impression that friends and relatives would step up with financial support, but that well came up dry. Most people had difficulty wrapping their heads and arms around the idea of a moneymaking business run by an African-American woman selling African-American books to African-American customers.

Instead, I supported myself by working as a psychotherapist, seeing one patient a day.

The Denver store was self-financed with $35,000 from savings from a partner and me, and it was imperative that we were careful with our start-up purchases. I don't remember buying anything new in the box. We bought used bookshelves and counters and repainted them and salvaged a cash register that had been discarded from a local grocery chain. The business was undercapitalized and we were operating on a shoestring budget, so all of the profit had to be reinvested to shore up the underlying finances. I came in with very limited knowledge about business finance, and my brother, a CPA who lived in another state, had no interest in doing a tutorial for his sister with this crazy idea of starting a book business. The fact that we had so little money yet were able to create a viable business is due in large part to my knowledgeable and patient accountant. He walked me through the financials and has remained my teacher throughout my years in business.

After four years I had established the business as creditworthy, which gave me the ability to borrow money to purchase the building that housed the bookstore and two other units. Since the money I was paying in rent was equal to my mortgage note and ownership brought in additional revenue from tenants, I had the numbers that showed I could service the debt. I had proven my ability to operate a business, and now would have the building as collateral, so I went looking for money. Still, it was difficult to attract investors, so we raised money for the down payment on the building from our customers, who became shareholders. They believed in us and had witnessed our growth and development and recognized the positive contribution to the community, so they were willing to invest. Once we demonstrated the store to be a successful business model, it wasn't a hard sell, and even my skeptical brother eventually became a shareholder.

. . .

When people talk about why businesses fail, money is often at the top of the list. From the start, most female-owned businesses are undercapitalized, which puts them at a distinct disadvantage. In the beginning, there are always mistakes; no one is perfect and there are bound to be missteps, but money ensures staying power. When money is tight, there is no wiggle room. This chapter will give you financial information and terms and tools to make you savvier when it comes to managing money and negotiating with lenders.

Money, they say, is what makes the world go around, and it's particularly true in the business world. Money is one of the most important, if not *the* most important, aspect of your business. When you talk about bottom line, you're referring to the foundation that keeps the doors open and your business operating. In this chapter I will focus on how much money you will need, where you will get it, how you will spend it, and how you will manage it. But first you need to know about your financial personality. Can you look at yourself objectively and describe your money management style? You need to understand who in your family manages the money and what is your comfort level with finances. Do you save? Do you spend? Do you carry balances on your credit cards? Make sure you know your credit score, which will show you the good, the bad, and the ugly. How you handle your personal finances is often an indication of what you will do in the business.

CALL IN YOUR SECOND SUPERHERO

When it's time to crunch the numbers and create the financial piece of your business, enter the *accountant*. When bombarded with an onslaught of numbers, the accountant is able to wrestle the most perplexing figures into submission. The relationship with your accountant is critical since the buck literally stops with them. The accountant compiles your financial records, does monthly sales tax reporting, and files your taxes at the end of the year, and it's your job to provide the accountant with the relevant information to help them help you manage the business.

In addition to keeping the books, your accountant can look at variables to identify and head off financial stumbling blocks, as well as counsel you about the various tax advantages and how they relate to the type of entity you chose for your business. He or she will recommend and set up the accounting systems so you can generate the necessary information for the reports. Often businesses use a payroll service, which not only manages the payroll and writes out the checks, but also keeps track of your monthly and quarterly payroll tax obligations. A real pothole that many small businesses fall into is not separating and paying sales and payroll taxes. When your business is registered in the state, taxes on your earnings are reported and these funds are collected on behalf of the government. All revenues are generally placed in an operating account from which you write checks. Never think that all this money is yours to spend. Rest assured that the governments will take what belongs to them. I created a separate tax account and regularly deposited the amount I owed for sales and payroll taxes so I was able to write the check when the taxes were due. The last thing I wanted was a padlock on the door of my business because of nonpayment of taxes.

Another pitfall is combining your personal and business finances or commingling funds. This is a definite no-no and doing so can cripple your business. As soon as you have funds that belong to the company, establish a separate bank account in the company's name. The payroll and sales tax account that I opened was a surefire way to be certain there would be no commingling. You must practice strict monetary segregation; sorry, no financial fraternization. The early establishment of a company bank account will make certain that personal and company funds remain separate.

You'll work closely with your accountant, who will keep your financial records and issue statements monthly, quarterly, and annually. Unless you are an accountant or are familiar with accounting procedures, your accountant will generate the documents. The goal of this chapter is to familiarize you with information and terms to facilitate your time with the accountant, but it is not an accounting lesson and should in no way serve as a replacement for professional services. An accountant can help you determine your financial needs, and provide a breakdown of costs involved in creating your business.

Your projections are based on a set of figures derived from two financial statements, along with a capital budget that you and your accountant must rigorously generate.

First is a *statement for the cost of start-up,* the money you expect to spend to start your business.

Second, *you'll use cash flow statements with ongoing expenses and anticipated revenue,* how the money will come into the business and be spent each month.

Last is a *capital budget,* the money that is spent on actual concrete things.

Since these figures are internally generated, many companies use accounting software like QuickBooks or Peachtree, along with a bookkeeper to keep records. Accurate, up-to-date books are a must, as they are part of your résumé when applying for a loan or line of credit, which is money the bank has agreed to set aside to loan you in the event you need it. You do not withdraw the money until you are ready, and you pay interest only on the portion you actually use. The "line" is for a specific amount with predetermined repayment terms. I used my line of credit in November when I had to pay for holiday items, and repaid it in January after the holiday sales.

The money you will require for your initial capitalization, including launch, is the start-up costs plus approximately three to six months' operating revenue. Most small businesses underestimate expenses and overestimate revenue. It's important to put aside that additional financial cushion in case no one is pounding down your door to buy your product or service during the start-up period. Another good idea is to factor in inflation. There's always a time lapse from conception to when you actually open your doors, and things rarely get cheaper. In fact, the cost of goods and labor is constantly escalating, so plan for these increases.

BUYING VERSUS LEASING

The comparison of the cost of buying an item or leasing it is a way to reduce cash flow early in the life of your business. Sometimes leasing will get you the asset with little out of pocket, but it will cost significantly more over the life of the asset than if you had purchased it outright. You will need to make comparisons for each item. Also shop banks and lessors, because each will use different rate and profit margins. Cash is the lifeblood of any business, but especially at start-up. Using secondhand, refurbished, or leased items are ways to conserve cash in the short term. Of course, these methods have their own disadvantages. If you need a high level of reliability for certain equipment, which may eliminate these options, you'll have to buy them new.

CALCULATING EXPENSES

The following is a list of basic expenses for your initial cash outlay. To get a solid estimate, you will need to go shopping. The best way to validate prices is to have at least three quotes. But the time between shopping and having money in your pocket may cause quotes to grow stale, so recheck them as you get closer to purchase. You'll incur many of these charges before you start your business, but bear in mind that most are one-time expenses.

There are three sets of estimates that are part of the planning process: start-up costs, capital costs, and operation cash flow. For each set, review Exhibits 1, 2, and 3 in the Appendix at the back of the book. They are from a mythical company and are examples of what the statements should look like. Exhibits 4, 5, and 6 are blank so you can insert your own numbers. The numbers are generated from the following list of expenses primarily for a retail business.

1. *Occupancy.* The rent or lease you pay the landlord for your business space. As you shop the marketplace, you will get a sense of the availability of comparable spaces and also a reasonable estimate of the monthly operating costs. There may be a one-time deposit of one month's rent and a damage-insurance deposit paid in order to hold the space. Included may be a clause that states this money will be returned at the end of the lease with adequate notice to vacate, barring any damage to the space.

2. *Utilities.* Light, gas, and water services and the one-time deposit necessary to put the utilities in your name and turn them on. Talking to previous occupants or the utility company will provide a reasonable estimate for this monthly operating cost.

3. *Telephone.* There are lots of plans, so look for one that will cap your phone cost. Some are all-inclusive, while others limit your long-distance usage. As you shop, you will need to have an idea of your local and long-distance usage to approximate monthly costs. Add to that, equipment you purchase or lease and a deposit to access phone service for the business that will be part of start-up costs.

4. *Inventory.* The goods you plan to sell to customers. It is the wholesale cost before the markup. And buyer beware, literally; I have found that retail entrepreneurs tend to overspend and blow their budget to stock the shelves. How much you spend should be based on how much money you have, what it takes to make the store look full, and the turnaround time of your vendors for replenishment. A key point is to contact your wholesalers to find out how the Internet will accelerate the delivery time. A speedy delivery time may lower the amount you need to stock. Inventory turnover is a key to selling things profitably. There is a cost to putting stock on the shelf and having it hang out there; it may get damaged with handling or go out of style, and sticky fingers may take a share. But with the Internet, FedEx, and UPS, you may be able to satisfy a customer as soon as tomorrow.

5. *Advertising and promotion.* How you'll let the world know you are launching. This cost is usually three times higher at the beginning, and you will need to research the costs of all types of media based on rate cards and demographic reach. For a grand opening, costs include ads and flyers, creating a website, and the development and printing of brochures. This is also incorporated in your marketing plan, discussed in Chapter Eight. The

start-up items above are different than the ongoing advertising and sales promotion that are part of your everyday operations.

6. *Business insurance.* Protecting yourself and business from liability. Shop around and get quotes from several companies to get the best deal. The cost of insurance is based on the particular type of business and the requirements of your lender and landlord. Most small businesses can use a boilerplate business owner's policy (BOP), which includes property, liability, criminal coverage, and various specialty coverage. You will need coverage for liability for claims brought for injury and damage to property that is leased, rented, or belong to a customer. Your annual BOP insurance premium is part of your operating costs.

7. *Business documents.* Licenses, fees, certification, and permits are often necessary. These can be the state, federal, and city requirements to do business in your area and the filing has to be done before hanging your shingle. Explore certification necessary for food service and special skills related to your type of business.

8. *Legal and consulting fees.* Fees charged by the accountants, lawyers, and professionals who assist in setting up the business. Examples include the lawyer who develops and files the legal formation documents, and reviews rental and leasing agreements and any contractual agreements; the accountant who sets up your books and assists in the number crunching; and perhaps a graphic artist who creates your logo and perhaps an architect to design your space. These numbers can be in both the start-up and operating costs depending on your need for ongoing services.

9. *Lease hold improvements.* Renovation of the space in preparation for occupancy. If you are not handy or don't have friends or relatives who are carpenters, you will need to hire contractors for the

remodeling, and to install wiring for lights and electronics. This may include the addition of heating systems, air conditioners, and water heaters, or just basic decoration and remodeling.

10. *Equipment.* Computers, software, and hardware to support your enterprise. Save money by buying an all-in-one machine that includes printer, fax, scanner, and copier. You'll need a cash receiver, which is now a computer-based cash register that sorts money and also manages your inventory and finances. For noncash payments, you'll need to subscribe to an electronic payment system and buy or lease a credit card machine. For retail, you may also need security cameras, and shelving for the storing and presentation of merchandise. These are all capital costs that will involve the purchase or lease of items.

11. *Furniture and office supplies.* Office furniture for your work space or back office can be purchased used or donated by friends and relatives. And don't forget your own castoffs that can be called up for duty from an attic or basement. Hold on to your money and remember cash is precious as you continue to complete your capital budget. Paper, pencils, and desk equipment seem small but can add up in the start-up costs; because they have to be replaced, they are therefore part of your monthly operating budget.

12. *Transportation.* The cost of purchasing a car or using your own vehicle for pickup and deliveries. If you purchase or lease a vehicle, it is a capital expense. Then add on an additional automobile insurance clause, which is a requirement when using a vehicle for business purposes.

13. *Signage.* Your banner of advertisement directing customers to your business or internal signage to help them navigate inside the space. Signage is considered a capital cost.

14. *Owner's draw.* The amount of money necessary to provide for the owner's personal expenses during the start-up. This is optional and only if there are funds available. Most of the time that is the owner's donation, and hopefully you have not quit your day job. The source of this money is operations, sales, or the line of credit. If it comes from using the line of credit, it's a bad sign.

15. *Operating capital for the first three to six months.* This money is a safety net to cover the differences between your estimated revenue and expenses and the reality that confronts you. Its source is a line of credit. Don't use it casually because it's what stands between you and disaster.

If you are starting an online business, you will not need to account for most of the above expenses, but you will need the following:

- Occupancy: the cost of preparing space to do business even if home-based
- Equipment: the purchase of computers, fax machines, printers, telephones, and furniture
- Consultation: the use of professional services for start-up
- Supplies: software, office supplies, and shipping materials
- Inventory: the cost of the goods you plan to sell
- Website: the costs stated in Chapter Two for the setup of your website, hosting, and ongoing maintenance

This is definitely a lot of data to calculate. It may be overwhelming to digest and apply to your business, but you can cut down on your legwork and save a few brain cells by contacting the trade group associated with your industry. By tapping into their network, you can access significant amounts of information, including start-up costs for individual business. You can also use your superhero accountant as a resource. Then take a shortcut on the Internet and do a search of your industry. You'll unearth a wealth of knowledge without leaving the comfort of home. My go-to resource was the American Booksellers Association, which had a book-selling school for prospective and current business bookstores. They had a complete checklist for start-ups, including costs for inventory, salaries paid to employees, and recommended vendors. Check online and you'll find that organizations exist for everything: real estate, beauty shops, restaurants, spas, and whatever. You name it, there's a trade group that supports it and is easy to locate online. Examples of some trade groups are National Association of Women Business Owners (NAWBO), National Restaurant Association, American Institute of Graphic Arts (AIGA), National Association of Home Based Businesses (NAHBB), International Special Events Society, and Independent Florists' Association.

Shannon Ayers Holden was equipped to deal with the money aspect but still had to overcome major obstacles to establish and grow her business.

The owner of Turning Heads Salon & Day Spa, Shannon comes to the highly competitive Manhattan beauty industry via an unlikely route. She is a graduate of Smith College, and earned degrees in economics and African-American studies. Before setting out as an entrepreneur, the Phoenix, Arizona, native had a successful fourteen-year run working at several Fortune 100 corporations, which served her well when it came to making the money deal for her salon.

Launching a major business, negotiating retail space, and financing a huge renovation is an intimidating endeavor, but Shannon came prepared, having already played hardball in the business world. She began her career as a system engineer and marketing rep for IBM in New York City and went on to work for Food & Wine *magazine as a district manager of sales. Three years later, she was lured to a major media company where she was a top sales performer; however, company accolades and a six-figure income could not prolong the obvious . . . she yearned to be an entrepreneur.*

Shannon had been a long-time client of Turning Heads, a ten-year-old beauty salon tucked away inside the YMCA in Harlem. During a phone conversation with a salon employee, she offhandedly mentioned that if the owners ever considered selling their business or taking a partner, she would be interested. She was pleasantly surprised to learn that in fact they were considering selling; so brimming with confidence and armed with good credit and savings, Shannon set out to learn all she could about the beauty business. She researched the industry and developed a business plan, and purchased the salon in 1995 by securing a loan for 80 percent of the purchase price, with the remaining 20 percent coming from personal funds.

When Shannon bought the business, there were only two years left on the lease, so going in she was already thinking about moving. She became more motivated after the landlord bestowed on her a stiff rent hike. Ouch! Shannon considered continuing to rent but moving to a different spot with street-level visibility, since her location inside the YMCA was less than ideal. Then she had a V8 moment—"Ha! I should just get a mortgage and own a place for the same amount I pay in rent!"

First, Shannon went hunting for a new location. She pounded the pavement, never finding the right property. But all the while, there was this corner building in her neighborhood that she would pass every day walking to work. Neglected and abandoned for almost twenty years, it had become one of the most notorious drug houses in the neighborhood. It was a complete train wreck, but she fell in love. Situated on the corner of a busy street, which made it an ideal location, the building had the potential of three income-generating rental apartments.

Shannon went to work to rescue the building. She sent letters to the owner's address that was on file at the Buildings Department but never got a reply. It was finally a random conversation with an acquaintance outside the building that set things in motion. Shannon shared with this woman her dream of buying the building to relocate and expand her business but said she couldn't reach the owner. The woman said she knew him, arranged an introduction, and within ten days they met and Shannon had an agreement to purchase. Next, Shannon worked to secure her financing. She had an SBA (Small Business Administration) guarantee on her loan through her bank to purchase the business, which she paid off early, so she approached the same bank to fund the next project. The new loan would be to purchase and renovate a building, and this time she was looking to borrow about ten times more than the first loan.

Screeching brakes! Not so fast. The owner wanted all cash and wanted to close the deal in thirty days. Impossible, since Shannon had to get money not only for the purchase but also for renovations. Reluctantly the owner agreed to ninety days to close, and to demonstrate her commitment to the seller and the bank, Shannon agreed to put up a 20 percent deposit instead of the required 10 percent, which she stood to forfeit if it didn't close on time. Of course, it didn't, and it was five months before the deal was done.

Once they closed, immediately the project was behind schedule and strapped for cash. But they sped, then limped along, until Shannon ran out of money, including her own personal funds. The building was only half finished, but she made the decision to move to the new location anyway, a year and a half behind schedule, because she was still paying rent at the Y. Then the bank decided to cut off her funds unless she could demonstrate the ability to cover the additional debt she requested with current business revenues, and the bank also refused to take into account the projected income from the three rental apartments that would eventually be finished.

For several months, Shannon was stuck, unable to finish the building and getting pressure from the bank. Eventually, her financial planner and friend came to the rescue by putting her in touch with another bank, which unlike her original lender was familiar with small business and urban banking. These banks have more flexible credit and collateral requirements and understand the need to provide creative solutions to fund fledgling businesses. The bank was opening in Harlem and looking for good businesses to invest in, so it was a perfect fit.

Shannon's story illuminates the difficulty of the construction process and how things never go as fast or according to plan at the beginning. It also speaks to the importance of the lender, and the necessity of finding one who understands your size and type of business in order to adequately fund your enterprise.

EXERCISE 1 • Time to get out the calculator and add up your expenses.

How much money will you need to start your business?

List and itemize your start-up costs. Refer to the examples and worksheets in Appendix Exhibits 1, 2, 4, and 5 to get a feel for the numbers and what a finished product developed by an accountant looks like.

GENERATING A LEDGER AND
ANALYZING A CASH FLOW STATEMENT

Compiling a cash flow statement with ongoing expenses and revenue projections is easier than it seems, since much of that information is in your start-up costs. Look at the list and identify what expenses will be reoccurring, like rent, utilities, advertising, telephone, credit card, insurance, and maintenance of equipment. Then add on any new month-to-month obligations such as payroll, taxes, dues, subscriptions, travel, entertainment, and debt service.

Next, you will need to estimate revenue, which is a projection of the money that you anticipate you will earn from the sale of your goods and services. The amount charged has been determined by your work in Chapter Two. If you have been charging for the products and services before formally going into business, it will be easier to determine how much more you'll make with increased effort put into your business. How many clients will you see in a day, week, and month? What is a reasonable increment of increase over a certain period of time? How many customers will purchase the products at your established prices? If you have multiple products and different prices, how many combinations will be sold for an average amount per sale? Revenues in retail can be averaged per square foot of sales space; an example of this is in Appendix Exhibit 3, and Exhibit 6 is a blank one for you to use. The cash flow statement demonstrates your ability to meet your obligations. It captures your debt service (monthly amount you owe) and any payouts regardless of the receiver. An example of a cash flow statement can be found in Appendix Exhibit 2, with a blank Exhibit 4.

> **EXERCISE 2** • This exercise addresses your bottom line according to your prices.
> Calculate your anticipated revenues and the breakdown of what you will charge for your products and services. An example of how to generate revenue is in Appendix Exhibit 3.

Once you are up and running, you can begin to insert your actual numbers for a more accurate understanding of how your business is doing. You can now generate a balance sheet and a profit and loss statement. The balance sheet is a snapshot that shows you where your business is at the specific time when the numbers are generated. It lists all your assets (anything that you have of value that you can turn into money, like your house, other property, or money market accounts) and liabilities (all of the bills, debts, or people you owe, such as credit cards, mortgage, and car note). By subtracting liabilities from your assets, you calculate the net worth of the business. A final financial report is the profit-and-loss statement (P&L), which determines if the business is making or losing money. The bottom line figure matches all of your sources of revenue generated from the sale of goods and services against your expenses that create the sales (this does not include debt service). This number can be positive or negative and is often referred to as in the red or in the black.

SHOW ME THE MONEY!

The next big question is: *From where and how will you get your financing?* Self-funding is always best, but most people don't have all of their start-up money available from personal resources. While many people draw from savings, equity in property, retirement accounts, and other tangible assets, there are considerations in the use of these resources based on individual financial, marital, and family situations. Your spouse's support of your enterprise might evaporate if it means forgoing that 42-inch flat-screen TV he's been eyeing. It is important for you to have a tight grip on your personal finances for two reasons. First, they are a foundation on which your business is based. If you are personally out of control with regard to how you handle money and personal debt, it's a reflection of your money management in business. Second, if you are seeking out lenders, they will always view your personal situation as an indicator of what they can expect from you as a business owner. They will infer from what they see as your personal record how soon or how likely they will be repaid.

Below I discuss the most common funding sources.

Cash Is King

Where can you get some cold, hard cash? If you've been a saver, congratulations, you're ahead of the game. But, unfortunately, the majority of Americans don't have a savings strategy. If you have some money sitting around in the bank with no particular use, this is the best option. But in the age of downsizing and company buyouts, some folks have walked away from their jobs with some cash and are thinking that this is the time to invest in their dream. Next on the money tree is something you can easily convert into cash, like your home or other property with equity in it. This is a good resource if interest rates are lower and your property has appreciated during the real estate bubble. It is low-hanging fruit if the property has appreciated and you may be able to refinance and keep your mortgage payments the same or lower. But don't bet the farm, literally. Stay away from any arrangement that puts you in jeopardy of losing your home if things don't work out. Another source of funds is life insurance. If it's whole-life rather than term-life, you can borrow against the policy; of course, make sure you restore it so that there will be money for your survivors in the event of your death. You can also tap into your retirement fund. Normally known as a 401(k), it's money you've set aside during employment, and sometimes your employer puts in additional contributions. Hopefully, you will be able to replace this money before you need it to retire and kick back on some exotic beach. We've all heard of entrepreneurs who have used credit cards to finance successful businesses. But what you don't hear about are the ones saddled with the long-term debt and high interest rates when they go under.

EXERCISE 3 • In this exercise, you'll have to account for your money and determine its accessibility.

How much money do you personally have, and where did it come from?

> How are you supported, and do you have dependents?
> How will you be supported during the start-up phase of
> the business?
> Review the personal financial statement in Appendix
> Exhibit 7 to develop one for your own situation.

Friends and Family

As mentioned in Chapter Four, friends and family can become involved in your business operations, but here we are speaking about them as investors. Regardless of the relationship with the lender, make sure you are clear on terms and whether these are loans, gifts, or investments. Don't be tempted to just do a handshake, but engage some written formality to spell out the terms, conditions, and repayment. Protect yourself from ever hearing these words: "All rise for the Honorable Judge Joe Brown here to decide the case of you vs. your friends or family." Court TV is not where you want to advertise your business. Parents are most likely to assist children with a gift to fulfill their dreams. Other relatives or friends may want a portion of the business in exchange for the money or want to treat it as a loan with or without interest.

Investors

Another resource is investors. They are people who will lend or give you money in exchange for commensurate ownership. Since the amount of ownership is dependent upon the money given, you must decide what percentage you are willing to relinquish and assign to it a dollar value. If it is a loan, do they expect interest and at what rate? Will the investors be involved in the business, making management decisions and sharing your passion and dream? You better know who you are getting in bed with, since this relationship is like a marriage and divorces are not pretty.

Venture capitalists are professional companies usually looking to invest big sums of money in large mature businesses. They expect the business to grow and provide a good return on their financing. The National Venture Capital Association offers for a fee a list of its members. The SBA-SBIC (Small Business Investment Company) stimulates the flow of private equity and long-term loans to small business. By completing a form, you can be added to a database available to the interested firms.

Most entrepreneurs have heard of "angel investors" and would love to be visited by those winged wealthy individuals or groups. Who would not want to be chosen by the most prominent angel, Oprah? Sometimes these investors find businesses when they are featured in magazines or newspapers. They make good loans at low interest rates and may specify a return after a period of time. They can also hook you up with consultation and technology assistance. Angels are kinder and gentler. But what if you are not out there in the public eye for them to find you? For this type of financing, you will need a good business plan to convince investors that you have a sound, moneymaking business.

Loans

Lenders can come in all forms and shapes: banks, credit unions, consumer finance companies, or commercial firms. Regardless of the financial institution that you approach for a loan, you will be required to complete a personal financial statement that gives a complete picture of your assets, liabilities, and any other financial indiscretion that you've swept under the rug. Review Appendix Exhibit 7, an example of a personal financial statement, which will prepare you for the information you'll have to provide to apply for a loan. As you will see, the financial statement is thorough, and the institution will want to know everything about your money, where it is, and what you're doing with it.

Your local bank or financial institution is a good place to start your inquiry about financing opportunities. They can be easy or difficult, depending on who you are to them, like a customer or just someone walking in off the street. The loan is based on their perception of your capacity to pay back the money borrowed. Some banks on their own have developed in-house programs targeted in low-income communities to reduce the stringent requirements for lending. The federal government has developed programs within the SBA to assist and to motivate commercial establishments to provide loans to small business. The best known is the SBA Guarantee, which will back up 80 percent to 90 percent of the monies the bank loans to a business in the event of a default. It is for borrowers who may not have the demonstrated capacity to repay from cash flow and inadequate corporate and personal assets to collateralize a loan. Also available are microloans that can be used for working capital, supplies, furniture, fixtures, machinery, and equipment. They are small amounts of money that can be under $100,000 but can extend above $1 million. The money is furnished by private nonprofit intermediaries serving communities in every state in the form of a revolving fund (as the loan is repaid the agency extends money to other qualifying businesses). The agency may require that you attend classes for technical assistance and complete a course to become eligible for funding. This type of requirement and ongoing support probably accounts for the

90 percent repayment rate. Information about the microloan programs can be obtained by going to the SBA website and clicking on the SBDC in your area.

Money for start-up businesses is never all that available, particularly in times of tight credit. It is the numbers game: the more research and effort, the more likely you are to succeed. You do not want to fail because of lack of trying.

To qualify for a loan, you are evaluated using the eight C's:

1. *Capital.* How much cash do you have, and how much are you willing to risk for your dream? This is your show, and risking your money indicates commitment.
2. *Credit.* What is your credit history, and what will show up when your credit record is pulled? You'd better know your credit score before anyone else, and if it's not good, fix it first!
3. *Collateral.* What assets do you have of value that can be quickly converted to cash if you default? This is also based on your net worth. If you have real estate, how much equity is in the property?
4. *Cash Flow.* How much revenue do you anticipate the business will generate to repay the loan? Is this a real number, or did you rub a magic lamp and make a wish? What is the sustainability of the business based on the business plan?
5. *Character.* How do you rate? Are you a reliable, trustworthy, ethical, and responsible person? Sometimes a lender may use your credit score to determine character.
6. *Capacity.* What are your experience, training, skills, and demonstrated ability to start and manage your business?

7. *Conditions or terms of the loan.* How much is the loan, and what are the terms? Will there be a guarantor? What is the stated purpose of the loan?

8. *Context of your proposed business.* How unique is your idea? What is the state of your business industry? How well have you assessed the competition?

Lenders will evaluate your eight C's from a complete and properly prepared personal financial statement.

YOUR THIRD SUPERHERO

Enter the *banker*, who has the power over the almighty dollar and the ability to bestow "cash money" to get your enterprise off the ground. Your banker can show you how to maximize your funds, offer financial counseling, extend a line of credit, and give you a description of the various banking products. The banker can also help you open a business account, which is important to keep you from commingling business and personal funds. You have to be able to determine the health of your business separate and apart from your own or your family's money.

A smart first step is to meet with the banker who handles your personal account and with whom you already have a relationship. If you don't have a personal bank account, open one now. A good credit history is a plus and can make the process of securing financing through your current banking institution easier.

Valerie Jo Bradley, owner of Harlem 144 Guest House, is a frugal home-based entrepreneur who used her house and its equity to help fund her business.

Valerie has converted her 1888 three-story brownstone in Harlem into a bed-and-breakfast, offering visitors to New York hotel-like accommodations with a personal touch. She had been a working journalist in Chicago with Johnson Publishing Company before moving to the Bay Area to pursue graduate studies. She was living in San Francisco and putting her master's degree in journalism to good use as director of public relations for the United Way, but she wanted a change of pace. She took her communications skills and moved to New York, where she served as Ambassador Andrew Young's spokesperson at the U.S. Mission to the United Nations, and later held various senior-level state and city positions. While at the U.S. Mission, she purchased her brownstone property for $36,000 in an undervalued market and during a period of inflation; this put her in an eviable position to capitalize on her investment. Valerie had a majority of the C's to qualify for the capital, which was a down payment equal to 25 percent of the purchase price. She came with a good credit rating, the property as collateral, cash flow from a job, and character references.

With the election of a new mayor, Valerie anticipated that her politically appointed job would became as obsolete as a subway token, so she negotiated a buyout to start her first business. With a $120,000 line of credit and the brownstone as collateral, she created a sole proprietorship (DBA), then known as the Bradley Group, a public relations and consulting company for businesses and not-for-profit organizations involved in community development and promoting black arts and culture. She was full-service, doing everything—annual reports, conference management, media placement, press releases, and business launching. Initially it was a slow go, but her rental income and line *of credit kept her afloat, and in three years the business became self-sufficient. Though the company was successful and turning a profit, it ground to a halt after a family crisis took her away from business for two years. Once the matter was resolved, her money was gone; she took a job until she was ready for another shot at entrepreneurship. Because she owned her home free and clear, she was able to obtain a mortgage, consolidate her debts, and start an LLC, Harlem Sole to Soul Tours, that provides historical walking and bus tours of Harlem. In 2005, having realized that the income cobbled together from tours, public relations, and event planning was not going to cut it, she converted her home into a bed-and-breakfast. While continuing to live in the two middle floors, with minimal renovation she transformed the upper- and garden-level rental apartments into three units of guest accommodations. This increased the revenues while reducing the aggravation of having long-term tenants. The cozy "suites" are decorated with personal pieces that Valerie has collected from her travels throughout the African Diaspora. The B&B is an attraction for international tourists who want to have a total Harlem experience by staying in a home, particularly a brownstone. And she provides a wholesome and healthy continental breakfast.*

Valerie has three home-based businesses under one roof, using all her skill sets and resources:

1. *Public relations and event planning. She has three or four clients, but the income fluctuates and is uncertain.*
2. *Bed-and-breakfast. The units have kitchens and bathrooms; the rack rate is $100 to $200 per night, with garden access for the largest space.*
3. *Tours. Although not independently cost-effective, they are offered for the benefit of the bed-and-breakfast guests as well as for corporate clients. The base rate is fifteen dollars per hour per person.*

Valerie hires employees as needed. A cleaning person comes weekly, but she handles most daily chores herself. She's started to network with the twenty other B&Bs in her area to handle their overflow and is expanding to book non-owner-occupied brownstones. She would eventually like to become a clearinghouse for bed-and-breakfast accommodations in Harlem. She is cautiously optimistic that the business will grow because the opening of a hotel in Harlem is not imminent and there is increased interest from European tourists.

Valerie has done limited marketing. Initially, she sent a full-page information sheet with pictures to her network and distributed her cards at retail establishments in the neighborhood; word of mouth has been effective. She plans to set up a website and do outreach to companies doing business in Harlem, such as hospitals and real estate firms, that may need client accommodations. With minimal expenses and overhead, she hopes, her revenues will reach $150,000 within the next year. Her biggest hurdles have been the winter heating bills and the seasonal nature of the business. The first quarter is as barren as the trees in winter, and she is attempting to save during the good times for the slow times. She is cautiously considering refinancing the property in order to access a $100,000 line of credit and reduce her 10 percent interest rate. However, Valerie is concerned because of the sliding economy and its impact on the foreign tourist market; any negative impact on the euro is a drawback for people coming to New York.

Valerie has set a good example of minimizing debt while maximizing assets. Instead of increasing her long-term debt and borrowing from external sources, she used the equity in her brownstone to meet her funding needs. She also demonstrates the importance of having a good credit rating and maintaining a positive relationship with one's banker.

> **EXERCISE 4** • Here you'll evaluate your credit worthiness.
>
> What is your indebtedness? What is your credit rating?
>
> Identify sources of funding (other than your personal finances) that you have sought and those for which you can qualify.
>
> Assess yourself on the basis of the 8 C's, and then rate your capacity for a loan from 1 to 5, with 1 being the worst and 5 being the best. Your personal financial statement can help you determine your rating.

The banker or investor will evaluate the validity of your business plan, the perceived quality of your estimates, and your ability to pay back the loan from business proceeds. In addition, the banker will expect you to provide a personal financial statement to show how you will pay the loan if the business fails. In the preceding chapters you've named it, claimed it, and explained it. And now, if you've done the exercises in this chapter, you've figured out how you're going to pay for it.

Chapter Six

Step 6

Location! Location! Location! Where Will You Put Your Business?

When I started to scout locations for the bookstore in Denver, I envisioned a spot central to my customer base. But with an African-American population around 10 percent and a community that was scattered and not in one specific locale, there was no clear traffic pattern for my customers. My store had to be a destination. I looked for a well-traveled street and came across an inexpensive two-story row house that could be adapted to retail with minimal renovation. Another plus was curbside parking, with additional space in the rear. I later purchased the building and became a landlord as well as a business owner, which cut my overhead.

Hue-Man II was located in the Harlem USA Retail Center just off 125th Street. It was prime real estate, smack in the middle of bustling Harlem, so there was heavy foot traffic. Rents in the area were steep, but I managed to negotiate a price that was far below market rate, and our payments didn't kick in until we opened for business. And to make the deal even sweeter, the landlord gave us significant lease-hold improvements.

When the unit was delivered, it was not just a basic vanilla box but had upgraded plumbing, lighting, and heating units. We got such great terms, in part because of community pressure about the lack of African-American small businesses located in the retail center.

This chapter is about selecting your space and the importance of choosing your location. You'll be spending countless hours in your new business, so this is one of your most critical decisions. You'll want your new environment to be comfortable and enhance your business, and this step will teach you how to identify your needs and evaluate your alternatives in order to pick the right space. If you are settling in a space separate from your home, think of the process and its significance as if you were shopping for a second home. Step 6 will also give you information on how to negotiate a lease with favorable terms and make the best deal in the short term or the long run.

The first thing to consider is the type of business you're planning. This will help you to determine how much space you will require, if a home-based operation is feasible, or if you'll need a separate location. Next, think about your customers. If they will visit you on site, you'll need space for display or separate rooms for other services. And ultimately the decision about location comes down to your needs, money, and what, if anything, you can afford to pay in rent.

EXERCISE 1 • This will further refine your thinking on your business activities and the square footage to be allocated.

Think about the nature of your business and write down the activities and functions of your operation (for example, sales, storage, food prep, treatment rooms, back office). Determine how much space you will need in total, and then designate space for any separated areas.

There are many different location scenarios, but what drives the decision is the type of business, availability, and, of course, money. The next section is a breakdown of some of the most common choices.

HOME-BASED

In the past, running an operation from home was thought of as the default choice for people who couldn't run a "real" business, but over the past fifteen years that perception has changed. A home-based business is no longer viewed as the "not so bright" stepchild but is now seen as a smart alternative to an off-site enterprise. Dentists, physicians, attorneys, hairdressers, caterers, financial planners, and other types of consultants are starting businesses from home. Some of the most successful and well-known businesses that started in home kitchens and garages include Hewlett-Packard, Apple, Amazon, Microsoft, and Carol's Daughter. Now, with the explosion of the electronic age, everyone has a computer and Internet access, so with a PC, fax machine, and some do-it-yourself office software, almost anyone can launch a business from home. With the World Wide Web, cyberspace becomes a virtual shop window for the sale of products and services without ever leaving your home. And why not? There are some big advantages to being home-based.

Home-Based Pros

For the risk averse, starting from home is a great way to dip your toe in the entrepreneurial pool without making a long-term commitment or spending your life savings. If your start-up money is tight, home-based has low overhead and can serve as a testing ground for you to refine and improve your concept and determine whether your business is actually viable. And at home, the commute is fabulous and the dress code is extremely lax (pj's and bunny slippers). Home-based businesses can be very family friendly; they're geographically convenient, and the flexible hours allow you to juggle family obligations and even keep your day job if you want to start out part-time.

Home-Based Cons

Of course, there are drawbacks to working from home, but with focus and planning they can be overcome. One of the main obstacles is the distraction. Typically you leave the house and go to a job where you're focused on work, but at home there's a house full of things to remind you of what else you could be doing. You might find yourself spending hours watching stupid pet tricks on YouTube, organizing your spice rack, or just plain goofing off by allowing all kinds of intrusions to interfere with work. Another problem is the lack of boundaries, i.e., not being able to separate your personal life from your professional life. You'll have to guard against the "time suck" of family and friends who'll phone or drop by unexpectedly and interrupt just because you're there and available. Be polite to friends, but keep it moving and let them know that you're working. Finally, working at home can be lonely and isolating. Work is a great place to detach from home life and meet and interact with new people. At home, you're there all by your lonesome. Start to worry if you've been sharing all your personal information with the UPS delivery guy, whom you now refer to as "girlfriend." Designate time as if you are going to and getting off from work, and get dressed as if you were leaving the house. Take an actual lunch break, and don't stock your house with fatty snacks: your fridge and cupboards filled with munchies will call out to you all day long to *"open me"* and *"eat me"*!

Here's a checklist of why a home-based business is the right choice for you:

1. You have enough separate space that won't intrude on your family's living area. You can see clients or customers and, if necessary, have a small reception area. There is space for office equipment, inventory, furniture, and storage, and you can add any special equipment necessary for your business type.
2. You can design and finance the physical changes in the home/work space to make it effective and efficient. It's safe and does not pose potential danger for family members, particularly if you have children at home. It is attractive to customers and clients if they come to your home as well as a pleasant working environment for you, and you've minimized the distractions.
3. The number of clients or customers who will come to the business won't cause a problem with your neighbors. You won't have heavy traffic in and out of your home, and the business won't have a negative impact on your community.
4. Zoning regulations will permit the type of business to exist in your area. The local, state, and federal zoning laws do not

prevent you from setting up shop in your residence with minimal signage.

5. You are eligible for the IRS home office deduction. If you use your home regularly, exclusively, and principally for your trade or business, you qualify. The IRS puts out a pamphlet that addresses how to apply for the deduction, how to calculate the figure, determine the deductions and expenses, and necessary recordkeeping. For more information, download and print IRS publication 587, "Business Use in Your Home."

Anitra Jones found that for her business, Aunt Ni Ni's Kitchen, there's no place like home.

Raised in a small town in North Carolina, Anitra remembers the smells and sounds coming from the kitchen. She grew up listening to her female relatives talk, argue, and laugh over food as they "put their foot in the pot" to concoct generations of mouthwatering recipes. It was within that homey space, sharing and bonding with her family's womenfolk, that Anitra developed her passion for food. But starting her own business would come later; her practical vision was to be an attorney. Anitra graduated from the University of North Carolina, but before going to law school she took a job at a law firm. That experience turned her off from studying law, and instead she went to work in the financial industry. She continued to cook at home as a hobby and even started selling cakes, cookies, and pies. She had previously earned a certificate in food preparation and during that time learned new kitchen skills at the Institute for Culinary Education, where she learned the art of cake decorating. In 2005, with praise and encouragement from friends and family, she decided to leave her full-time job to start her business.

By keeping her focus and finding a "sweet" niche, Anitra has turned Aunt

Ni Ni's Kitchen into a thriving home-based baking business specializing in desserts like cakes, cookies, pies, and cupcakes. Anitra was able to start her business with a relatively modest $30,000, largely because she didn't have to pay rent. Instead, she converted the basement of her family home into a commercial kitchen by putting in a standing mixer, professional stove, convection oven, large sink, worktable, and commercial refrigerators, most of which she bought used to save money. There was also room for a small office and storage space. Her home, a four-story town house, is located on a quiet residential street, and her business is a destination and directed to specific customers who come to pick up the products. Customer traffic is sporadic and does not call her neighbors' attention, who, by the way, are also customers. There is no external signage or prohibitive zoning regulation.

Anitra makes reliable, tasty, well-prepared, and professionally presented products that are baked to order, which is how she beats the competition. By not carrying inventory, her product is fresh, guaranteed homemade, and the customer knows whose hands have touched the baked goods. She gets the majority of her business through referrals from satisfied customers and positive word of mouth. She bakes for individuals, restaurants, and private events, and does both retail and wholesale for local restaurants that don't have baking facilities or prefer to outsource their baked goods. Her formal marketing is limited and is basically just business cards and a brochure listing products and prices, which are considered reasonable. Her new specialty, wedding cakes, will expand her reach since they come with a built-in marketing component due to each cake being seen and tasted by at least a hundred people. And because each one is unique, wedding cakes give her the opportunity to tap into her creative side. Anitra gets intimately involved with each personal purchase, particularly the cakes, and she is considering adding event planning with additional products and services. Her goal is to replicate her corporate salary, but she has no plans to develop a retail outlet. She would like to start a family and wants to keep the business manageable and flexible so that she can be a happy stay-at-home mom.

Anitra's business is self-contained and efficient. She was able to add baking equipment without disrupting her living space. Because she bakes to order, she doesn't need separate areas for displays or customers to browse. By operating from home, Anitra dramatically reduced her operating costs and proves that home-based can be a big success.

EXERCISE 2 • Refer to the checklist on pages 115–116 when answering the following questions:

Is your business conducive to a home based *operation*, and if so, why?

Describe your home, location, and community.

How you would organize the business space within your home?

So now your home-based business is up and running and humming along. You're making money and feeling secure and you let out a contented sigh. But what's that crying in the background? Looks like your baby has outgrown its crib. It's time to consider moving your venture to a commercial space to enhance it and allow it to flourish. Have you anticipated and planned for this expansion? Do you have sufficient current and projected revenues to cover rent and additional expenses?

COMMERCIAL SPACE

There are three main reasons to consider renting outside space:

1. The business was never conducive to being home-based.
2. Your home-based business has expanded to warrant additional space.
3. The business is retail with continual customer traffic, and it requires setup with display cases for products, plus storage, deliveries, and checkout.

Ask real estate professionals and they'll tell you that the three most important factors in choosing a space are location, location, and location. Before you start perusing the rental section of the newspaper and sign on with a real estate broker, first do your homework to expedite the search. Commercial space is expensive and carries many additional costs like insurance, utilities, and leasehold improvements, so you want to get this right.

Location evaluation requires knowing what you need and what the various options have to offer. This section will help you to explore the variables in selecting your space.

Start with the following business location checklist:

Customers: Are they geographically close and centrally located, or are they spread out? Will you have to go out and find them and drive them into your business? How much of your target population do you need to support your business, and is there a large enough pool of people with your customers' characteristics? There's more on customers in the next chapter.

Competition: Are there similar types of businesses near your location? Sometimes it's an advantage, but generally it's best to be miles from your competition so you're not all chasing the same dollar.

Traffic: Where are the centers of activity? What kind of traffic does your business need, and does the location have natural traffic?

Transportation: How are people traveling? Are they walking, using public transportation, or driving? Is there adequate parking, with meters or a lot? Is it on a main bus line or subway route?

Visibility: How will you stand out? Can customers find you? What kind of signage is permitted to advertise your business and help customers locate you?

Zoning: Is the area properly zoned for your usage? And don't write off suburban neighborhoods. There are often opportunities for commercial businesses in residential areas with restrictions.

Appearance: Does the surrounding area feel safe and inviting, and does the space project the appropriate image for your business?

Rent: Is it within your budget? We will discuss this in more detail later in the chapter.

History: How has the property been used in the past? Were previous businesses successful, and if not, why?

Vendors: Will you need to locate near suppliers of any materials necessary to run the operation?

Labor force: Will you need employees, and if so, is there an adequate pool of qualified people?

Neighboring businesses: How will they affect you? Qualify the businesses that are around your chosen location by determining whether they enhance, detract from, or are neutral to your business. Evaluate them on how they look, how they are managed, and what their customer base is.

MALLS AND SHOPPING CENTERS

Shopping centers and strip malls are often magnets for small businesses because they can bring steady traffic and are professionally managed. The downside is that rents tend to be higher than detached retail, so you're paying for that easy access and traffic. Landlords may inflate their numbers about the hordes of people who shop at their outlet, so do your own on-site evaluation to get a feel for the demographics and actual number of shoppers. Also, take into account how many stores are vacant and how long they have been unoccupied. To make sure you're getting what you pay for, strike up a conversation with other tenants, who will hopefully give you inside information about maintenance and management.

Veronica Jones has learned and relearned her lesson about location.

Grandview, a prophetic name for a store that has had several changes of view and venues, has been Veronica's education in the importance of location. She worked for ten years learning about the business of fashion and retail as a contemporary sportswear buyer for Gimbels in New York and Joseph Magnin in San Francisco, then returned to New York and became vice president of sales for Gina Ewing Bis and Kenar. She then established the Veronica Jones Showroom, which represented new designers in the contemporary sportswear market. While representing designers, she followed her dreams and opened a retail clothing store in Nyack, New York, in 1987. The charming river town, with no fashion shops, was a prime location. The population was diverse in race, income, and lifestyle. Most of the existing shops specialized in gifts, antiques, jewelry, and arts and crafts. Grandview would introduce grand style to Nyack.

The store was 1,200 square feet in area, with 800 square feet of sales space. Veronica funded the endeavor with $25,000 of her own money and kept her day job while her niece ran the store. Grandview built a loyal customer base of upwardly mobile women with an average income of $60,000, many of them mothers and daughters. Business was good. Five years later she decided to add a second location and opened a store in New York City. But success was short-lived. When the stock market crashed and the overall economy slid south, her business took a hit and she closed the second store.

The Nyack location continued to flourish, but Veronica still dreamed of having a boutique in Manhattan. Her wish was granted in 2001, when a space became available in Harlem. While the new location was not on a well-traveled street, it was on a main thoroughfare and seemed full of potential. The rent was reasonable for the 800 square feet, and the space was adaptable. The Uptown Grandview was embraced by newly minted Harlemites and was featured in the local fashion press. The store did $140,000 in the first year, and Veronica seemed on her way to creating another successful venture. Then came 9/11 and the bottom fell out again! Businesses across the board in Manhattan took a hit. The loss was particularly rough for African-American women, many of whom lost their jobs or had a decrease in salary. Discretionary income shrank and folks were hard pressed to part with that hard-earned dollar. Her sales continued to drop and she closed the store in 2006.

Veronica had to do some soul-searching and evaluate her locations and where she generated the most revenue. She is now concentrating on her original store, and sales have tripled. The store is located in the downtown section of Nyack, where she has a five-year lease and pays $2,000 per month in rent, with a 5 percent annual increase. Nyack is one of several small villages located next to other cities that also deliver customers. The commercial strip is populated with quaint, *eclectic shops, and is a shopping destination positioned to attract tourists. There is street parking and a parking lot, and the merchant association is active in scheduling events such as street fairs and festivals to generate traffic. Although business is good, Veronica has recently been forced to face the fact that although her clothing is cutting edge, her operating systems were as outdated as linebacker shoulder pads. Veronica made a major overhaul and switched to a modern computer-based system for monitoring sales and tracking merchandise and will finally add a website. The "grandview" is for her business to do $1 million. Now that she is in the right location with loyal customers, Veronica will take her business into the twenty-first century with technology and hit her money goal.*

Veronica's story shows that sometimes a promising location when examined more closely can have serious drawbacks. Although Veronica had "uptown aspirations," her Nyack store proved to be her most successful location. The clientele is steady, surrounding businesses are supportive and not competitive, and she has a favorable lease.

BUSINESS INCUBATORS AND BUSINESS CENTERS

When choosing a location, there are two other options to consider: using a business incubator, which is typically not-for-profit, and using a business center or executive suite, a for-profit enterprise.

A *business incubator* is a large facility divided into smaller spaces for fledgling companies to launch and grow during their vulnerable start-up period. It's a protected environment where business people can do manufacturing, cooking, and office work, and see clients. There are also specialized centers for food services and for technology companies that develop software for games and education. The owners share the cost of the common space and services with other businesses; this can reduce maintenance costs and financial anxiety. Incubators not only offer a physical space, but also provide technical and financial assistance and network opportunities that can save you countless hours and dollars compared with going it alone. Many are operated by government agencies; for more information, contact the National Business Incubation Association at www.NBAI.org. It provides thousands of professionals with information, education, advocacy, and networking resources to assist early-stage companies worldwide.

Business centers, also called *executive suites*, are run by companies that own, lease, or rent large spaces divided into offices to rent for a limited period of time. They are typically used for short-term rentals and are ideal for displaced or downsized businesses or start-up companies seeking space without the commitment of a long-term lease. The space may be completely furnished, and may be open or enclosed, and such services as Internet capability, receptionists, mail delivery, and phone-mail services may be provided. Depending on the type of business, many offer such specialty services as screening facilities lounges and conference rooms.

Consultants and businesses providing professional services are often a good fit, since office suites are one-stop shopping for space solutions. The spaces range in size; they can be as small as 25 square feet, with room for one person with a one-desk operation, or as large as hundreds of square feet, with room for multiple offices and equipment. In a depressed economy, this type of niche real estate market tends to stay strong. During periods of downturn, start-ups want to minimize the usual expenses and commitment, and can take advantage of shared services and arrange favorable terms. The costs, which can be as low as a few hundred dollars a month, depend on location, size, and services needed.

As an engineer, Josie Umoh took a very practical approach to meeting her business needs. Through a business center, she found the most direct route to set up shop and have access to services.

Josie Umoh started her company, Apex Engineered Solutions, in a business center in Dallas. She is part of a growing industry that provides general services in engineering and technology. For the engineering services, her customers are large engineering firms that require mechanical, electrical, and plumbing design support for roadways and commercial buildings, hospitals, hotels, and airports. For the technology, she offers operations, desktop, customer, and system-monitoring support.

Josie's story seems to reflect the American dream. Her parents came to the United States from Nigeria to obtain advanced degrees; Josie and her siblings were born in the States. Even as a child, Josie was logical and linear in her thinking. She graduated from Ohio State University with a B.S. in industrial systems engineering. After graduation she followed a job to Dallas and subsequently completed a master's of science in management and administrative sciences at the University of Texas at Dallas. For the next seven years, she worked for Dannon (food manufacturing), Sanden International (compressor manufacturing), and Saber (airline reservation systems). She also freelanced and did contract and consulting work that nurtured her entrepreneurial spirit.

In 2001, Josie ventured out on her own as a sole proprietor with $30,000 in savings and one employee. She rented an unfurnished office in an executive suite; the landlord provided phone service, conference rooms, office support, copiers, mailing service, coffee, and a reception area. For Josie, it was the perfect choice and an easy space solution for a start-up business with uncertain revenues but needing a professional presentation. She was overly optimistic, however; although she had excellent technical skills, she was lacking *in business expertise. She expanded prematurely, and when her money ran out, she borrowed from friends, tapped her retirement, and sold her rental properties. Her initial business model did not factor in the downturn in the economy or the duration of the sales cycle for her services. She moved her offices to another executive suite and worked on her business development skills. She also registered and became certified with the city, state, and federal government. As her business grew, it was much easier to expand using business centers, since she could better focus on tasks like marketing and expanding services without having to worry about her logistics and providing services to support her business. The business was not without its challenges, but it was still able to grow, and in 2008, with several years of steady revenues and a solid client base, Josie moved into her own commercial space.*

Today she has a staff of twelve, and in 2009 she opened a new office in Washington, D.C., to try to capture more federal business. She went after new contracts after doing research that indicated that 50 to 80 percent of money spent by the federal government (namely, the Department of Homeland Security) is with companies located close to the White House. For the satellite office it made sense to use what had worked in the past, and she operates out of an executive suite with shared services.

Josie has a unique and lucrative skill set, but her challenge was to turn that into a successful business. Like many entrepreneurs, she expanded too quickly and had to go back and learn more about the business end, and determine how her services could be applied to a larger *very* profitable industry. This helped her recognize the support services she needed. Instead of trying to chase down all the components, she wisely took advantage of an easily accessible product packaged and offered through business suites.

EXERCISE 3 • Does your business require commercial space, and if so, why?

Rate your commercial location based on the business location checklist. Also, consider Veronica's example and the criteria she used to decide on a location for the Grandview and the things she learned about her customer base.

Once you've decided to rent or lease the space, it's time for the rubber to meet the road and negotiate the deal. This is a legal binding contract, so it's best to have an attorney work with you or, at the very least, review it before you sign on the dotted line.

POINTS TO CONSIDER WHEN YOU BEGIN NEGOTIATING THE LEASE

Rent is one of your biggest expenses, so be a tough negotiator to keep it as low as possible. Usually, rent is based on the square footage, and the larger the space and sometimes the longer the lease, proportionally lower the price.

- Check out the cost of rent near your location for comparable space. For the comparison, you will want to use the annual or monthly cost per square foot. The square footage cost is obtained by dividing the annual rent by the square footage. For example, monthly rent of $4,000 × 12 payments per year equals

$48,000, and divided by 2,000-square-foot space is equal to $24 per square foot.

- A guideline is that occupancy expenses should be between 10 percent and 20 percent of your expenses. There are, however, many variables based on whether the space is a stand-alone or within shared space.

- Airports are an example where the rent is often in the 20 percent range because it includes advertising done by the airport, unbeatable traffic, and maintenance provided for the common space.

- Freestanding space may be less costly, but you'll spend more money directing people to your business as a destination, so rent depends on the benefits to be delivered by the landlord. Dissect the figure to determine what is actually included.

There are various kinds of rental agreements, and various conditions to consider:

Fixed rent is a flat amount you pay monthly for the space, which generally includes specific annual increments.

Percentage rent refers to paying a specific percentage of your revenue for rent. This can be a good deal if the percentage is reasonable, since your rent is based on earnings. When your earnings are low, so is the rent, but then your landlord benefits from increased earnings.

Fixed and percentage rent is a combination of both. You start with a small flat rent and pay a percentage after your earnings reach a certain, predetermined threshold. This guarantees the landlord a fixed amount with the possibility of more based on the success of the business, so you and the landlord share the risk.

Guarantors. Many landlords request a guarantor for the lease. This makes you personally liable for the payment, and places your personal assets at risk, so it is best to avoid this exposure if possible.

Utilities. You might have to pay for things like electricity, gas, and water, so ask to see previous bills or request an estimate from the local utility company.

Incentives. If the landlord won't budge on the rent or pay the utilities, ask for incentives. The most popular is free rent for a specified period, but there can be other inducements, like help with refurbishment and additional maintenance services.

Starting date of the lease. The best deal is for the clock to start ticking when you open for business and start to make money. Some landlords want rent to begin when you take possession of the premises, so you are paying during renovations, which always take longer than anticipated.

Length of the lease. Typically you'll try to lock in for a longer period, particularly if you're getting a good deal upfront. Time frames vary between one, five, and ten years. Sometimes people think that a shorter term is better, as it gives them time to see if the business will work. The problem is that at the end of a year or two that you are at the mercy of the landlord, who can price you out of the market.

Incremental rent increases. The amount and time frame for rent escalation should be calculated for the long run. A low beginning rent can be deceptive because over the years, if you're successful, the landlord can demand huge increases and overcompensate for a "teaser" starter rate.

Termination or bailout provisions. How can you break the lease before the termination date? What are the penalties and conditions? Many leases are written with the total amount owed for the length of the lease, but you may be able to sublet or negotiate to bring in another tenant.

Contractors. They are a breed unto themselves, and once they get started, you generally have limited control over how fast they work, regardless of what they tell you in the beginning of your project.

Condition of the premises. The costs of getting the place ready for business are called leasehold improvements. Since it's the landlord's property that you're enhancing in value, ask him for money or assistance to help pay for the expense. Get an estimate of the cost of the improvements to have when bargaining with the landlord.

Security deposit. The amount of money you put down in the event of nonpayment of rent and to ensure that you give adequate notice for the termination of the lease can be a flat rate or one or two months' rent. The money is held in escrow and returned at the end of the lease provided all conditions are met.

Restrictions. These are any limitations or prohibitions that would cause conflict or impede you in your ability to conduct your business.

EXERCISE 4 • You can use the above criteria to decide whether the terms are favorable and whether it's in your best interests to sign.

Review your lease and compare the terms to each of the above points in negotiating a lease.

By considering the type of lease proposed, the dimensions of the space, and rent to be charged, you can calculate the cost of your space per square foot. Then factor in an estimate of additional charges, like utilities and any add-ons or incentives, to get a more complete picture of what the space will cost you.

PURCHASING A FACILITY

The best-case scenario is usually one where you can buy the business space. However, what matters is not only having the money to purchase but also external variables such as property prices, credit availability, and interest rates. With ownership you are your own landlord and have more control over your occupancy costs. Most important, as we've seen in previous examples, it's a way to build wealth with an asset that, hopefully, will appreciate over time. Owning creates wealth; renting does not. At the very least, with ownership you'll have a piece of collateral to use when borrowing funds. The process for purchasing a facility is essentially the same as for leasing space. You will need a commercial real estate agent, preferably one who specializes in investment sales brokerage, since you'll need help with financing. But brace yourself for the sticker shock and get ready to hand over a down payment of 20 percent to 30 percent, which is probably not realistic for most first-time entrepreneurs. In addition, once you find your ideal spot, the owner of your dream location may not be looking to sell. If the property is on the market, buying will start you off saddled with enormous debt unless you have deep pockets.

EXERCISE 5 • If you are considering purchasing the space, go back to the business location checklist and evaluate the space using those criteria.

YOUR NEXT SUPERHERO

The *architect*, the personal magician who has the ability to transform a hovel into a haven, is the person who will design your space and make it not only inviting but also functional. Particularly important for a retail business, an architect will design service areas, storage, and back-office space so they flow. Your architect will also help develop the security systems, deal with the building codes, and create a personal ambience that reflects your signature style for your business.

EXERCISE 6 • Make a drawing of the space. Don't worry; even if you are not an artist, do your best with your own free rendition. Scope out where you want to place the things you will need in your space.

Congratulations! By completing the exercises in this chapter, you have conquered "space." Not the *Star Trek V: The Final Frontier* kind, but the material entity of what started out as your intangible idea. You now have a physical image of what your business will look like and where it will be.

Chapter Seven

Step 7

Know Thy Customers: Who's Buying What You're Selling?

I got information from the American Booksellers Association that identified my customers as predominantly middle-class women between
the ages of twenty-five and fifty. Naturally, my product was directed to
African-Americans. Although the numbers were small and dispersed in
Denver, I believed I had a great market, since the black population had
proportionally one of the highest percentages of middle-class residents
in the country. Based on this information, my marketing strategy targeted potential customers who looked like me . . . so I was completely
surprised by who came through the door. It was working-class folks who
learned about the store through word of mouth. My patrons were not
whom I'd expected, so I had to go back to the drawing board and gather
more demographic information, and not necessarily in the areas that I'd
targeted. I realized that I was selling a cultural product and I needed

customers who were culturally connected. They were strivers, both white and blue-collar workers with middle-class values, who emphasized reading and education, particularly for their children.

The Harlem store was an entirely different landscape and customer base. The target population was half a million people with an annual income of $30,000 in a densely populated area in close proximity to the store. So while the income was higher in Denver, the number of residents in Harlem was five times larger. And what I learned from the Hue-Man in Denver was also true in Harlem, that my most loyal customers were the working class, not necessarily the middle class. Add to that Harlem's deeply rooted history and appreciation of the arts and culture dating back to the Harlem Renaissance.

Once they came through the doors of both stores, we knew how important it was to keep track of our customers, so from the beginning we collected names and addresses in a visitors' book. We got even more detailed information at the point of sale from computer software on the cash register, which captured how often and what people purchased.

Customers are your lifeblood and your livelihood. Grasping this fundamental truth means recognizing that the customer comes first in business. This chapter is devoted to learning everything you can about your customers and how demographics and specific characteristics influence purchasing decisions. Step 7 will show you how to identify your target market, how to appeal to them, and how to court them to capture their retail dollars.

WHO WILL BE BUYING WHAT YOU'RE SELLING?

Once you've clearly defined your goods or services, you need to target your customer base. You may have a brilliant business idea, but never forget it's customers who put money in your pocket. You need to put a face and personality on your customers, including demographics like age, race, and gender so you can best determine how to reach them. Your job is to get to know who they are, their interests, attitudes, and values, with the goal of first getting people to walk through your door, then to keep coming back, and finally to tell friends and family. It's not enough to hang your shingle and wait for the random passerby; you have to tailor a strategy that will distinguish you from your competitors to pull people in and create repeat customers. As you probably know, this selling tool is called *marketing*. It can make or break you during the start-up phase and is critical to the ongoing growth of any business. The more thorough your knowledge of your target market, the more effective you will be in influencing them to give you their business.

Angie Hancock had a rose-colored vision of Harlem but encountered a few thorns along the way.

Angie believed she knew her potential customers. After all, they were Harlemites and she loved Harlem. Her mission was to spread the love, and she wanted people who live, work, and visit Harlem to fully embrace the bounty of the borough. Her goal was to drive customers to the rich variety of food, entertainment, services, and shopping that were available uptown, so in 2006 she launched Experience Harlem, a business designed to "brand" the neighborhood.

When it comes to branding, Angie is a well-seasoned pro. She received a bachelor's degree in accounting and an MBA in marketing in her hometown of Chicago. Angie did a nine-year stint as a brand manager for Sara Lee before moving to New York in 2003 to work in marketing for Ann Taylor. It was there that she began to hatch her business plan. First, she secured housing by buying a condo—in Harlem, of course. Then with her small savings, she started a home-based business, capitalizing on the fact that Harlem had become the hot, new community with people moving into luxury condos, renovating brownstones, and renting new apartments. New businesses were sprouting up overnight, and newspapers and magazines were shouting about the revival of the Harlem Renaissance. Despite the proclamations, Angie's research and observations uncovered information about her clientele and their customers that represented significant challenges to get them to patronize Harlem and spend money in their own backyard.

- *Even with the influx of new residents, the income level of Harlem's population remained relatively low at around $35,000.*
- *Many of the new businesses were undercapitalized and had little money for marketing.*
- *Businesses lacked the skills to implement marketing concepts.*
- *Businesses continued to have difficulty overcoming the residual negative images about Harlem being a run-down, unsafe area.*

With this unique customer information, Angie took the brand, Harlem, and offered its burgeoning businesses reality-based consultations and affordable products that would mesh with the brand image and demographics. She bundled the business together to offer lower rates on the advertisements under the Harlem banner, and offered a book of redeemable coupons so whatever was offered could be measured when customers used them. The businesses cross-promoted each other and developed cooperative relation-ships and assisted in developing low-cost individual and business promo-tions. This hands-on approach instilled trust, confidence, and willingness to participate.

Angie has also had her own challenges. She launched her business with enough money to get up and running, but after seven months she had to resort to credit cards and dip into her retirement fund to carry her until she could cover her expenses. To pay the bills, she does consulting in the corporate world and anticipates that it will be several years before the business turns a profit. Her primary product is a stylish, colorful guidebook of Harlem busi-nesses that includes special offers and discounts. She supplements this with ExperienceHarlem.com, a website that lists businesses and provides loca-tions, photographs, and a description of their offerings. She consults with her clients to determine their individual marketing needs and assists them with cross promotion and cooperative arrangements. While it has been a struggle, Angie is still high on Harlem and one of its best promoters.

Angie came to understand that despite an idealized view that she and others had of the marketplace, the hard facts and consumer behav-ior told a different story. She had to reevaluate her approach and meet business owners and their potential customers where they were in the moment and not where she envisioned them to be. Then based on their needs, she had to come up with a marketing strategy. Just as she had to earn their confidence and loyalty, business owners had to earn the same from their customers. What Angie demonstrates is the importance of learning to manage expectations, which in her case meant starting with a marketing plan initially focused on creating a strong foundation and then later working on business growth and development.

IDENTIFYING CUSTOMERS

In order to create an effective marketing strategy, you need to first distinguish between the two types of buyers, on the basis of usage:

End users: Those who actually consume or use the product or service.
Channel users: Those who serve as a conduit to the end user.

For example, if your business is selling cupcakes, the end user is the person who eats them and the channel user is the coffee shop or bakery that sells your cupcakes to the consumer.

There are different markets for the two types of users. If you are selling your cupcakes directly to the customer, the cupcakes are likely to be consumed immediately and you receive all of the money the consumer pays for the cupcakes. For the channel user, the cupcakes will be purchased in quantity and displayed on the shelf before being purchased and eaten. The cupcakes need to be priced for wholesale, or at a 50 percent discount from the baker, in order for the store to make a profit. Self-published authors are an example of people who are trying to reach both channel and end users, since they sell books directly to readers and also wholesale to bookstores.

Potential, New/Existing, and Exiting Customers

In addition to usage, there are three basic types of customers:

- *Potential:* When you're starting out and before you've opened for business, you will focus on the potential customer because that's all you have, since you don't know who will walk through your door. You'll speculate about your customers and try to use resources to find out what you can about them.

- *New/Existing:* What you know about your existing customers will depend on the information you collect on their first and subsequent visits. Later in this chapter I'll discuss the kind of information you collect because your goal is to keep them coming back.

- *Exiting:* The exiting customers are those who have patronized your business but whom you have not seen over a long period, and you want to know why. You can send a reminder that you're still around, or if the numbers are small enough, you can give them a call. Sometimes they have moved, shopping with you has become inconvenient, or they're just no longer into you. Periodically purge your customer list, but it would be good to know why a customer is no longer coming so you can work on areas that need improvement.

Finding Out Who Your Customers Are, What They're Like, and Where They Are

Initially you'll have limited customer information, so your job is to learn more. First you have to find your customers. One way is by purchasing lists from entrepreneurs who have purposefully collected names intended for sale. You can also buy names from national publications. Peruse the newsstands and just make a list of the ones that are relevant to your product, service, and market. By using zip codes, you'll generate a more specifically targeted list segmented by demographics and location. But before you put out cash for a list, do some research to understand exactly what you're buying and if the list is current or relevant to your market. The data from national publications can be hit or miss and may not have the best information for your particular area, so a better way is to contact local publications like your neighborhood weekly community magazine or those that target specific professions or areas of interest. Their lists are much cheaper, and if you're lucky or charming enough, you might be able to persuade someone in your industry to let you use their lists for free. Pricing is generally based on the size of the list and the popularity of the publication. On the positive side, purchasing a list is easy. The downside is that it's expensive and difficult to determine the list's effectiveness. The seller will promise you a gold mine full of thousands of eager buyers, but this is rarely the case, and you don't know it's a bust until you've spent hundreds of dollars for half a dozen responses. Regardless, you'll still need to determine your demographics to provide the list servers with some direction so that their information will match you to your customer.

Treat your potential customer like your new BFF (best friend forever). As you're getting to know them, try to figure out who they are, if they're like you, and what would make them dump you for a new BFF. Or maybe they're like a family member, a friend, or someone in your network. Think about yourself in relation to them and in what ways your business impacts their life. How does your product or service fit into their lifestyle? Is it something that they'll use daily? Is it a basic need, or is it discretionary and purchased after the essentials are taken care of?

As you pinpoint your target market, pay attention to the following demographic statistics and trends that will affect your customer base.

- *Age:* The age of buyers is getting younger, with a new concentration on preteens, who are creating fashion trends and spending money like mad. In the past, marketers disregarded young people, but that has changed dramatically as we realize the influence young people have on their parents as well as having their own money to spend. On the flip side, the elderly population is increasing. People are living and working longer, with more disposable income. Aging baby boomers have created a whole new market for services and products that target their health care needs.

- *Income:* If your product or service depends on discretionary income, there's an upper tier of very wealthy consumers who want high-end items. Conversely, there's huge opportunity for selling goods and services in lower- or working-class undervalued inner-city neighborhoods. According to Social Compact Inc., a nonprofit coalition of business leaders committed to promoting successful investment in lower-income communities, their studies show that residents they surveyed often spend disproportionally higher amounts for basic and discretional items according to their income. These emerging markets have anomalies and opportunities that have been overlooked in traditional marketing strategies. However, during an economic downturn, nonessential purchases are the first to be cut.

- *Education:* People with higher levels of education often have higher levels of income and also more specialized tastes based on their educational experience. As more workers are getting specialized training beyond high school, particularly in computers and high-tech fields, their tastes have also elevated and may be more representative of a higher class.

- *Ethnicity:* Certain businesses lend themselves to niches where there is a basic product but directed to a particular ethnic group. The African-American bookstore is a prime example, since the industry is bookselling, with the business directed to

African-Americans. As businesses go global, there will be a need for language skills, and being bilingual, particularly in the Asian markets, is a huge advantage.

- *Gender:* We women know the difference between the genders. Overall, women read more fiction books for entertainment. Men value empowerment, information, history, and biographies about men with a masculine image, as in suspense and legal thrillers.
- *Occupation:* Different types of jobs require skill sets and training as well as attracting certain types of people. You may be able to identify an occupation that meets your demographics and thus has a captive market of consumers. Think about businesses that provide goods and services to prisons, which is unfortunately an expanding market.
- *Household size:* Money spent on entertainment definitely varies by family size. If there are children at home, their needs are vastly different from a single-person household.
- *Marital status:* Trends show more single women and unmarried couples living together spend significant amounts of money on leisure activities and nonessential items. Their spending is often tied to maintaining a certain appearance and status.

Liz Spear loved her work making beautiful showpiece garments. She found a locale full of people who would recognize her artistry and, more important, buy her clothes.

Liz Spear of Liz Spear Handwoven creates unique handmade garments from cloth she weaves on a loom; from the beginning she knew it was all about the customer. She understood that her product was a specialty item and that she needed women, and a few men, who could appreciate her hand-crafted one-of-a-kind clothing. In order to find a network and customers, she moved to North Carolina, the heart of America's "craft country," where she would try to establish her niche business.

Liz has always enjoyed working with her hands, weaving or making pottery. She received a BFA from St. Cloud State University in Minnesota, majoring in pottery, and leaned toward creating rather than teaching. Pottery suited her practical nature and offered an opportunity to create functional art instead of sculpture. She worked for a ceramic company and perfected her throwing skills (making pottery with a wheel) and business skills. The company had a small group of potters who worked as independent contractors, and in her middle-management position she handled product development, inventory, sales, and marketing and learned all aspects of the business.

Even working with ceramics, Liz maintained her interest in weaving. She collected looms, fabrics, threads, and yarn, and made rag rugs that she sold to friends and family. In 1991, she purchased a more complicated loom and realized that weaving at home was more satisfying than her pottery work; after twelve years she decided to concentrate on her passion. To improve her skills, she entered the Professional Crafts Program at Haywood Community College in North Carolina, one of the most respected schools for teaching arts and crafts. She completed the program in three years, developed a business plan, and prepared to establish a business as a sole proprietor. While Liz was quite confident about her weaving and creative abilities, she recognized that if she wanted to succeed as a self-supporting independent contractor, she would have to fortify her shy personality with some salesmanship and people skills. This involved selling not pots but garments, which are much more personal—they touch the skin and reflect an individual's personality. Teaching at craft schools gave Liz the opportunity to interact with students and staff, and to improve her people and promotional skills. This inspired her to broaden her base. She joined three regional professional craft organizations that held nearly a dozen fairs a year, with 100 to 200 vendors and 3,000 to 6,000 attendees. The organizations provided networking opportunities and immediate entrée into the craft community along with business development opportunities.

Liz knows that her uncommon clothing demands exceptional customers. She describes her customers as mostly over-forty professionals with disposable income to purchase high-end exclusive garments. These are people who don't want mass-produced items, who are looking for unusual handmade shirts and jackets that are comfortable and easy to care for. Their numbers are highly concentrated in the South, where there are year-round craft fairs. About half of her customers are repeaters, and many are her peers, fellow craft artists. Tourists make up the other half. They buy because they want something to take home that reminds them of their trip. When her clothing is worn at fairs, it attracts attention; that buzz and word of mouth are her main marketing tools.

The garments, which include tops, skirts, and coats, are priced between $300 and $450. Liz weaves only about two hundred yards of fabric a year, so each piece is labor-intensive and rare. She does very little wholesale, and her primary revenue stream is from craft fairs and from placing garments on consignment in select boutiques. She attends six to eight fairs a year and sells ten to twenty garments at each fair. To reduce expenses, she shares a booth with another artist who is a dyer and uses silk fiber for accessory items. Their collaboration has resulted in new and creative designs, which enhance sales and keep the product fresh by adding new dimensions to their work. Liz has recently purchased a computerized loom, which allows her to make more intricate patterns; these have been a big hit with her customers.

Annual revenue for Liz Spear Handwoven is $44,000. Although her *income is modest, Liz loves her work and happily manages as a single person with a simple lifestyle. If sales dip, she can supplement her income with educational demonstrations. The weaving demos are done in stores that sell her garments, and often end up converting some customers into weavers. Liz has an informational website but no plans to expand into online sales. She feels her clothing needs to be seen, touched, and tried on to be fully appreciated. When you talk to Liz, you feel her sheer enjoyment from the making and selling of her clothing; she equates this with sharing herself with each customer, and that brings her fulfillment and satisfaction.*

Liz's story is the opposite of "Build it and they will come." Instead of setting up shop and trying to draw customers in, she sought them out by going to where they congregated. She knew that her clothing appealed to a very specific type of customer with discriminating tastes, and she wasn't going to find them hoping for walk-in traffic at a static storefront. Liz identified her market, then created a business model in a location that put her in the direct path of her customers.

MARKETPLACE TRENDS AND THEIR INFLUENCE ON YOUR BUSINESS

Information on marketplace trends is important, as they either positively or negatively affect your business and can allow you to predict behavior to expand your customer base. The increased age range of customers, on both ends of the spectrum, gives you a wider and more diverse clientele. Technological innovations like cell phones and the Internet allow you to reach markets faster and cheaper, as well as increase the mobility of your businesses. Everything is faster. Movies transport you to another place and pack a lifetime of action into two hours. Television makes everything move almost at the speed of light, and international commerce gives you access to customers all over the world. It's more than just technology and cold statistics; it's also lifestyle information, which represents the intangible aspect of the buyers, and this includes:

- *Religious beliefs*. As traditional church attendance has declined, there is an increase in large megachurches that are nondenominational, with members identifying themselves as spiritually connected. Products and services that enhance spirituality, like Nature's Nuggets mentioned in Chapter Two, can have much more appeal to this population.
- *Political beliefs*. There are identifiable characteristics based on political party affiliation. This was never more apparent than in the 2008 election. How many references did you hear to the younger and technically savvy who voted Democratic and the red state persons who represented more rural and isolated communities.
- *Entertainment*. People are spending a huge amount of money on a wide range of entertainment, with music topping the list. Portable music has almost become a necessity. Music is everywhere; just check out the number of iPod earbuds sprouting from people's heads. Books are another example, in part because of the accessibility of literature. Although there's been a decline in independent bookstores, books are available at Wal-Mart, Target, and even drugstores.
- *Travel*. Not only is there an increase in the number of travelers, but they are searching out exotic places and using more varie-

ties of transportation. There is great interest in travel magazines and special travel sections of newspapers, offering advertising opportunities.

- *Food preferences.* Eating organic, healthy, and vegetarian are continually being promoted and getting more visibility, which is matched by our national obsession about obesity and weight loss. For example, a dance studio or Pilates lab that has special classes for the overweight and offerings of special recipes for healthy living can capitalize on this phenomenon.

- *Values and morals.* There is more discussion and concern about one's core beliefs, which influence thoughts and behavior and ultimately consumerism. Going Green, with its commitment to minimize climate change and preserve natural resources, has impacted the cars we drive and how we dispose of our trash and carry out groceries. This provides opportunities to identify products and services to focus on those needs and interests.

Knowing the above not only influences your products or services, but also assists in their location and ways to market to them.

CONDUCTING RESEARCH

On your mission to become better acquainted with your consumer, one way to gather information about end users is by performing primary or secondary research. If you want to get information directly from the source, you can do your own survey. Some business owners simply pass out questionnaires on the street or at places like churches or clubs, where people congregate. Others have gone to secondary sources like the local librarian, who has a wealth of resources and free information at her fingertips. She can direct you to publications provided by the Census Bureau and the Department of Commerce and local, state, and federal government agencies that can supply information relative to your area. The Internet has tons of services that allow you to access business data free or inexpensively. If you're a student, colleges and universities have research departments either independently or within a business school, and many educational institutions have entrepreneurial departments. Finally, check out trade and professional associations. For a typically nominal membership fee, you'll enjoy member benefits and receive insider information, current data, and technical assistance.

Take Names and Make a List

On Day 1, when you open for business, collect the names of your customers. Customer lists are one of the least expensive yet most valuable tools in developing and evaluating ongoing marketing strategies. Start your list by having a book or cards available for the customers to sign in. They'll appreciate your interest and look forward to hearing from you. Get their name, address with zip code, phone number, e-mail address, and how they heard about the business. Having the address and zip code helps you see where the customers are coming from and the areas you're reaching. Many retail software programs that are tied to your sales and inventory systems will maintain your customer database. They can record visits, amount spent, and items purchased. By tracking the customers, you will know frequency and the date of their last visit, which allows you to identify frequent buyers, big spenders, and those you need to reach and touch. You can also develop programs to reward as well as notify customers by sending an alert when new products of interest are available. How they found out about the business lets you know the effectiveness of your advertising and assists in targeting your marketing.

EXERCISE 1 • This exercise takes your stick-figure rendition of your customer and turns it into a well-drawn portrait.

Describe the demographics of your best customers: age, sex, income range, and social class.

What else do you know about them? For example, any details you could flesh out, like lifestyle, shopping habits, and social values.

Why did you pick them as your best customers?

Where did you get the information?

How many do you estimate are out there, and where are they located?

Tell Me What's On your Mind: Conducting Your Own Focus Group

Start with what you know about your customer and add on information gathered from organizing small groups to discuss your products or service. These are known as focus groups, and researchers charge big bucks for the service, but you can do it yourself. For the Hue-Man Bookstore, I invited a group of friends and neighbors to my home, and over sandwiches and dessert they discussed the books and cards I planned to sell. For sharing their thoughts and opinions, I gave each one a box of note cards as a gift. This also works great if you're selling food and beverage items and you can make samples and host a tasting. From their interactions in the focus group, you can determine the likelihood of them as buyers and ambassadors. My participants became the source of my initial mailing list. The following is an example of a pre-opening survey.

We are interested in opening a wine store in your area and want to know about your wine purchases.

1. Do you live in this area?   ☐ YES   ☐ NO

2. Do you work in this area?   ☐ YES   ☐ NO

3. How often do you pass by this area?
   ☐ Weekly   ☐ More than once a week
   ☐ Monthly   ☐ Several times per month

4. Do you enjoy wine?
   ☐ Yes, and I purchase bottles of wine.
   ☐ Yes, but I do not typically purchase wine outside a restaurant or bar.
   ☐ No, I do not drink wine.

5. How often do you purchase wine or other spirits from a store?
   ☐ Weekly   ☐ More than once a week
   ☐ Monthly   ☐ Several times per month
   ☐ Two to four times   ☐ Annually
      per year

6. Where do you purchase wine?
   ☐ Wine store   ☐ Liquor store
   ☐ Supermarket   ☐ Internet

---

7. Do you have a favorite store from which you regularly purchase wine?
   ☐ Yes ☐ No

8. If yes, what do you like about this store?
   ☐ Location ☐ Price ☐ Wine selection
   ☐ Service ☐ Other _____

9. What type of wine do you purchase? _____

10. How much do you typically spend on a single store purchase of wine?
    ☐ Up to $20 ☐ Up to $50 ☐ Up to $75
    ☐ Up to $100 ☐ Up to $150 ☐ More than $150

11. Do you also purchase spirits? ☐ Yes ☐ No

12. How much do you spend?
    ☐ Up to $20 ☐ Up to $50 ☐ Up to $75
    ☐ Up to $100 ☐ Up to $150 ☐ More than $150

If you would like to be contacted regarding our store opening and promotions, please provide the following information.

Name: _____

E-mail address: _____ Telephone # ____-____-____

Mailing address:

Address_____

City_____ State_____ Zip Code_____

Thank you for taking the time to complete this survey.

A simple survey can also be effective with existing customers who have knowledge of your business and can give you more specific information about your products, customer service, and marketing. Below is a sample survey that can be used to gather demographic information and determine utilization and satisfaction, depending on your particular needs.

Sample Satisfaction Survey for Mollie's Sweets

TELL US ABOUT YOURSELF

Name _____

Address _____

City _____ State _____ Zip Code _____

E-mail address _____ Telephone # ____-____-____

Which category best describes your age?
☐ 16–19   ☐ 20–24   ☐ 25–30
☐ 31–49   ☐ 50–64   ☐ 65+

What is your marital status?
☐ Single   ☐ Married   ☐ Divorced

Sex   ☐ Male   ☐ Female

Are there children living in your home?   ☐ YES   ☐ NO
If yes, what are their ages? _____

What is the highest level of education you have completed?
- ☐ Less than high school
- ☐ High school diploma or GED
- ☐ Some college
- ☐ Associate's degree
- ☐ Bachelors' degree
- ☐ Master's degree
- ☐ Doctoral degree

What is your occupation?
- ☐ Employed full-time
- ☐ Employed part-time
- ☐ Stay-at-home parent
- ☐ Full-time student

Which category describes your annual household income?
- ☐ Less than $30,000
- ☐ $30,000–$39,999
- ☐ $40,000–$69,999
- ☐ $70,000–$99,999
- ☐ $100,000–$149,999
- ☐ $150,000 or more

DESCRIBE YOUR EXPERIENCE WITH MOLLIE'S SWEETS

1. How did you hear about Mollie's Sweets?
   - ☐ Passed by Mollie's Sweets.
   - ☐ Mollie's Sweets was recommended.
   - ☐ Mollie's baked goods were served at an event I attended.
   - ☐ Other _____

2. How long have you been purchasing baked goods from Mollie's Sweets?
   - ☐ First time
   - ☐ 1–4 months
   - ☐ 5 months to 1 year
   - ☐ More than 1 year

3. How often do you purchase baked goods from Mollie's Sweets?
   - ☐ Weekly
   - ☐ More than once a week
   - ☐ Monthly
   - ☐ Several times per month
   - ☐ Several times per year

4. What is your favorite treat from Mollie's Sweets?
   - ☐ Cookies
   - ☐ Cupcakes
   - ☐ Pies
   - ☐ Cakes

(continued)

---

5. With whom do you share your favorite Mollie's Sweets treat?
   - ☐ Children ages 1–5   ☐ Children ages 6–12
   - ☐ Teenagers   ☐ Adults younger than age 35
   - ☐ Adults ages 35–54   ☐ Adults age 55 and older

6. How likely is your next purchase of baked goods to be from Mollie's Sweets?
   - ☐ Unlikely   ☐ Somewhat likely
   - ☐ Likely   ☐ Very likely

7. How likely are you to recommend Mollie's Sweets?
   - ☐ Unlikely   ☐ Somewhat likely
   - ☐ Likely   ☐ Very likely

8. How convenient is it for you to purchase from Mollie's Sweets?
   - ☐ Not convenient   ☐ Somewhat convenient
   - ☐ Convenient   ☐ Very convenient

9. Rate the following from 1 (most important) to 5 (least important).
   I choose to purchase my baked goods from Mollie's Sweets because:
   - __ It provides the best-tasting baked goods.
   - __ The baked goods are homemade.
   - __ The level of customer service is high.
   - __ The prices are good.
   - __ Other

After this chapter, you should be *this close* to your potential customer. You'll know what is important to them and why they would buy what you are selling. With that information, you can tweak your marketing strategy to inspire them to become loyal patrons who come often, spend money, and spread the word.

Chapter Eight

Step 8

Calling All Customers: Getting the Word Out to Bring Them In

My vision of how I wanted the store to be perceived started with our name and logo. Originally, I conceived Hue-Man as a multicultural concept with books representing all races. I planned to start with what (I thought) I knew, African-American, and then add Latino, Asian, Native American, and nonethnic best sellers. I had no desire to use my personal name; the thought of hearing it day in and day out would work my last nerve. So I looked for a word or words that represented the multiethnic nature of the business. Having worked in human resources, I started thinking about "human" and woke up in the middle of the night with the word "hue." The dictionary defined it in terms of shades and colors, so I compounded it into Hue-Man, meaning man of color. And although I let go of the multicultural aspect, the imagery still worked, since we come in all shades. The original logo had four profiles in black, white, yellow, and brown, with a red stripe down the center. When color printing was too expensive, the logo was depicted in black, white, and shades of gray.

In Denver our initial marketing had no specific funding. Whatever I could scrounge together I used to pay for flyers and to run ads in the local African-American newspapers. I bartered for radio spots with free books and sent out press releases that generated only minimal interest and response. Mostly, I got referrals from my network of friends and lists from organizations where I was a member. By collecting in-store names and customer information, I learned that people had heard about the store through word of mouth, and most of my business was not from my originally targeted middle class. Many of my customers came from churches, inspiring me to change my marketing focus and run announcements in African-American church bulletins, using an "Each one bring one" campaign. To attract the middle class, I had to figure out what they valued. These folks were strivers who were "movin' on up" and they wanted "the biggest and the best." I decided to promote the store as the biggest and the best African-American bookstore. Since Denver already had the largest independent bookstore, the Tattered Cover, the media picked up on the theme of Hue-Man as the largest African-American bookstore in the country, thus branding the store.

After we opened, the first years were tight, so our direct advertising budget was still limited and we had to maximize every dollar. We bought space in local newspapers, magazines, and weekly, monthly, and daily publications, which included coupons. When they were redeemed, we wrote the amount the customer spent on the back. This gave us a general sense of the effectiveness of the promotion and helped us make smarter advertising choices. Another way our business grew was through my affiliation with the American Booksellers Association. I joined as a member before being elected to serve on the board of directors. Since I was such an active participant, they supported the store and me. I positioned myself as an expert in African-American literature and became the go-to person to find out the trends in African-American stores. I eventually formed an African-American segment, with two hundred active members, within the American Booksellers Association. I took a "train the trainer" course and became an instructor at a bookselling school, teaching the modules on finance and marketing. I later developed and taught a segment for African-American booksellers.

Early on, Hue-Man held book signings featuring writers. Publishers took notice of the largest African-American bookstore, and it became a place to send authors. It wasn't easy. Denver is not a big stop on the touring circuit and doesn't have a large African-American population, so by piggybacking with the Tattered Cover, we could offer two book signings for authors coming to the area. We printed a monthly calendar of events for in-store and local distribution and sent it out to customers. Local newspapers also wanted to know about the author signings. The calendar and its spin-offs yielded the best bang for our marketing buck. We also selectively sponsored events and donated free books, and our customers responded and appreciated how we enhanced the black community.

Hue-Man in Harlem required less effort since it was more about extending the brand. Our landlord, Harlem USA, featured the store prominently in all of its promotional materials, and local and national media continued the buzz by running articles about what was hot in Harlem and writing features before and after the opening. Whenever I had the opportunity, I talked up the store with local and national organizations that invited me to speak. We celebrated the opening with a party attended by Maya Angelou, Stevie Wonder, Ossie Davis, and Ruby Dee. We collected customers' names and e-mail addresses and always asked how they learned about the store. We used the list to communicate regularly, keeping customers informed about events and author signings.

It's time to tackle marketing, which is often the last thing an overwhelmed entrepreneur thinks about but the very thing that can provide the tipping point between success and failure. This chapter will show you how to brand your business and use every element from your name to displays and even casual interactions to project an image and promote your enterprise. It will also cover promotional strategies, including the various types of advertising and how to make them work as part of your marketing mix.

Newly minted entrepreneurs often operate under the mistaken belief that "if you build it, they will come." But unless you are offering money or free food (and for that matter, it better be good food), it's up to you to motivate people to beat a path to your door. Marketing is the way that you tell customers about your product or service and its availability. It is also how you work to position the business to find a unique place in the market so that it can rise above the other types of products and services that vie for attention and recognition.

WHAT'S IN A NAME?

It all starts with the naming of your business. Your name and logo are often the first thing the customer will see, and first impressions are important and lasting. They are the visual representation of your business and should draw attention and be an illustration of your enterprise and the image you want to convey. You want to be easily remembered, so the name should not be too long and the words you choose should in some way reflect the type of business you're in. The name can't be used by some other enterprise, and you can check on availability with the Secretary of State or local government in the jurisdiction where your business is organized. Even if it's not taken, to avoid confusion, steer clear of names that sound or seem familiar. Spend time testing the name and logo on people. Ask them what they think and what the name brings to mind, and don't rush into anything. It's like your package label, and once it's out there it is hard to take back.

Read through the following names, and consider their effectiveness in conveying the nature of the business.

James Pipes (plumbing): Clear and direct. James is the owner's first name and "Pipes" is associated with plumbing.

Associated Business Supplies (office supplies): Not bad for an office-supply business, but "Associated" doesn't convey additional meaning.

Fannie's Bookstore (retail children's bookstore): Good use of the owner's name, which sounds also like a child's name.

Here Comes the Bride (wedding cakes): "Bride" is a specific reference to a wedding but not related to food, so the name is not as clear as it could be.

BethJames Consulting Group (husband-and-wife computer consulting): This is a fusion of the first names of the owners and could work if there is some name recognition within friends and family and the customer base.

Sweet's Cookies and Cakes (sweet baked goods): Quite specific, and the first word is a descriptive—but it doesn't really say anything other than that the product is sweet, which is assured with "Cookies and Cakes."

Maid to Order (house-cleaning service): Very good representation of the business and good play on words.

EXERCISE 1 • In past chapters you've claimed it and named it, but now you'd better be able to explain it.

Write the name of your business, and explain why it was chosen.

Describe or draw your logo, and discuss how it represents your business, product, or service.

Using what you developed in Chapter Two, write a description of your business that will go on your printed material and advertising. Make sure you use language that will convey the proper tone. For example, if you're aiming for a top-shelf image, stay away from words like "bargain" and, instead, use words that evoke luxury and status. Be creative but not confusing, and don't be so clever that people won't know what you're selling. There may be a short and a long version, depending on where you plan to use it.

ADVERTISING, PAY TO PLAY

The most direct way to get the word out is through *advertising*. It is a "pay to play" way to tell your prospective customers about your business. In other words, you pay directly for print space or airtime. Your advertised message should be simple, straightforward, credible, truthful, professional, and informative. Don't forget to include crucial information like how to find you. On the plus side, advertising is direct and specific, but it can be expensive, so do some legwork since all ads are not created equal. Before you plunk down cash, be a discerning buyer and research the media outlet to determine if the ad will get the desired results.

Look at their *demographics* to determine if the customers they reach are the ones you want.

Review the *publication time* or *broadcast airing schedule* to get the largest reach for your customer demographics.

Request *rates cards* and *cost sheets* to review the best price points and if there are any discounts for frequency or by bundling packages.

Using this information, you can make cross-media comparisons to find a mix that's within your budget.

Hello, Can You Hear Me? How to Track Your Ad

Once you've made the buy, it's important to come up with a method to track the effectiveness and customer response to your advertising so you'll know what worked and what was a bust. One way to measure is by offering a discount or a small gift if consumers mention that they heard about you from a specific media source or if they bring in a copy of the ad. When the ad coupons are retrieved, tally the redemption rate and note how much was spent. As a general practice, I would greet and talk to customers and always ask how they heard about the business. Although it wasn't a scientific measure, it gave me a feel for how well the marketing was working.

The following are the most common forms of advertising, and their pros and cons.

NEWSPAPERS

Pros: The daily newspapers reach a large audience in a short span of time, and copy is quickly and easily changed. The material must be concise and camera-ready. Placement is key, front versus back or near a featured article or frequently read column. Weekly, local community newspapers, and special sections often offer good rates and target specific markets and demographics.

Cons: The downside is that they have a short shelf life. It's a one-shot deal, and you have to compete for the reader's attention and stand out from headlines, featured stories, and other advertising. You can compensate by placing more ads and getting a frequency discount and by being creative in presentation to make your ad stand out.

MAGAZINES

Pros: Magazines offer the ability for placement in specific geographic and demographic markets with regional editions. Smaller trade magazines can reach targeted markets with more reasonable rates. They help build credibility and prestige and have a high quality of presentation and longer shelf life. The best resource for finding smaller publications is at newsstands. When I advertised mail-order books in *Essence* magazine, I received very few orders, but for years people would proudly tell me how they saw the bookstore represented in *Essence*. Although this visibility did not turn into immediate sales that I could track, this helped build name recognition. Sometimes it's difficult to immediately measure results, as it may take many references and repeated exposure to your business to prompt a sale.

Cons: Often overlooked by small business because ads tend to be expensive since they are in color. Major magazines, which do less selling and more branding and image building (and a small business needs sales), may not be best for small businesses.

RADIO: There are two types of formats, music and talk. When considering an ad buy, tune in to the broadcast to decide if it would appeal to your customer. Then match your business with complementary programming and look for a tie-in. Try to find a hook to motivate the host to pitch your product or give you a guest spot to talk about your business and answer questions on the show. If you never thought of yourself as a radio personality, put on your best Aretha Franklin voice and give it a try. With so many local productions it can be easy to get on. Practice those sound bites and keep the comments brief, informative, and concise, since time flies by when you are on the air.

Pros: They're targeted, since they're typically local and reach a preselected audience. You can barter for time and spots and use your product or service as an incentive and a tool for trading or giveaways to the audience.

Cons: It is relatively expensive and copy must be brief, and it needs to be repeated frequently to have an impact. Presenting at nonpeak hours, however, can reduce the cost.

TELEVISION

Pros: Producers are always on the lookout for content. If you are on the radar, they may just find you, or you might be able to get airtime on segments that feature small businesses or are about your product or service. Don't forget cable. Stations need to fill time, so it pays to check in your area for local and public-access channels.

Cons: Although major networks have an enormous reach, most likely their price range is out of your reach; seconds of TV ad time is measured in millions of dollars.

YELLOW PAGES

Pros: It's the most inexpensive and widely used form of advertising. In print or via the Internet, people use the Yellow Pages to locate businesses and get information on products and services. Back in the day, you had to let your fingers do the walking since the Yellow Pages was the only place to find addresses and phone numbers. While print is still available, more and more people are using the mouse to scamper over the Internet to pull up maps, reviews, and other detailed information. The cost of a print ad is based on a standard or display size and goes up depending on how much you want to stand out from your competition.

Cons: Advertising in the Internet Yellow Pages is free, and there is pressure to pay for bigger and bolder displays to stand out or pop up.

EXERCISE 2 • Completing this exercise will help you determine your ad budget.

Describe the advertising media you have selected and explain why.

What is the approximate cost for each one selected?

What is the information or content for a newspaper or magazine ad?

What would you say about your business in a one-minute radio or TV spot?

OTHER INGREDIENTS OF YOUR MARKETING MIX

In addition to direct advertising, there are other ways to promote your business that require less money but more time and creativity. The following are some inexpensive promotional ideas that, when combined, can be a big boost to your sales revenue.

- **Business cards.** Don't leave home without them. Give them out at events and to anyone you talk to; on the bus or subway, pass out those cards. You are not working it unless you're giving out five to ten a day. You'll be surprised at how much information you can fit on the front and back of a business card, but don't bombard people with trivia. Keep your card simple and uncluttered. The layout should include the business name, address, phone and fax numbers, your name and title, website address, e-mail, and logo. If the nature of the business isn't obvious from the name, state it clearly on the card. Not everyone may get what your business is from your clever name.

- **Brochures.** You can pick from one-, two-, or threefold depending how much information is necessary to convey your message. Resist that urge to fill every margin with content, which will make it look busy and sloppy. Keep it sleek and professional, with white spaces, color, and photographs. Brochures are excellent handouts in addition to business cards, and can also be placed in advertising bins at visitor and information centers. You may be able to create your own brochures using software packages that walk you through the process.

- **Flyers.** They're a low-tech, high-impact, extremely effective way to convey a special event. They can also be used for basic information to pass out at large venues like street fairs and cultural events. Find places where your customers congregate, like other noncompetitive local businesses, beauty and barber shops, health clubs, and places of worship, to let people know who you are and what you do and where they can find you. Pick a busy, popular street corner or transportation hub and pass out your flyers to pedestrians. Think of flyers as a mini-billboard, and don't be afraid to use color to make a bold impression. They can also be reused in your business as takeaways.

- **Newsletters.** They give information about events, sponsorships, new products, and industry breakthroughs. They can be a teaching tool, advice column, and have a gossipy tone. You can throw in bits and pieces of anything that would be of interest to your customer. Newsletters can be mailed or distributed at the business and offer added value and can just be a nice touch when offered to a walk-in customer.

- **Website.** A must-have instrument in your marketing toolbox because it does so many things for you and requires less cash in comparison to other forms of promotion. You have to get on board the cyber marketing train because everyone will ask if you have a website, and if you don't, you lose all "street cred." A website gives you the opportunity to reach millions of potential customers around the world at minimal cost. Depending on your objective, you can build it as an information site with a slick and simple design, using text and pictures. Start with images and copy from your printed material and add on bells and whistles. If you plan to sell online, you'll need a shopping cart where customers can place merchandise they've selected to buy, and provide a secure method of payment and shipping options. There is software that allows you to track your customers to determine frequent buyers and big spenders and, above all, to get those e-mail addresses; they are a great way to send out mass announcements. If you're computer savvy, you can build it yourself. If not, hire someone and learn the process so you don't have to call the Geek Squad every time you need to refresh and update. Ask around for website developers and look at sites you like for ideas. Remember, imitation is the sincerest form of flattery, and you don't need to reinvent the wheel.
- **Packaging.** There are two types. One is the container or wrapper for the product. This is the first thing the customer sees when the product is on display, and it continues to have an impact after an item is purchased. It must be functional, appealing, eye-catching, and generate interest, with name, logo, and information on the

package or label. The other part of packaging is what the customer transports the product in after purchase, so it will also be seen by others. Create a bag that people will covet, and make sure you have some form of identifying information like "I Shop at [Your Store Name Here]" right on the bag. You can design trendy reusable bags, which can be sold at cost, with the colorful logo, store, and business details that will serve as a walking advertisement.

Getting the Word Out Through Social Networks and Blogging

Although social network sites do skew toward a younger demographic, don't automatically write them off as an online hangout for slacker kids. The name itself can be deceptive, but social network sites aren't just about socializing; they're also about networking and building professional relationships. They are a way to bridge the gap between social and business environments, which is important, since a lot of business takes place in social settings. Online social networks allow prospective customers to make a more personal connection with a business and its owners and products. It changes the interaction and takes your business out of a sterile setting and makes it more human and user-friendly. By using tools and applications of social networks, you can take a tired marketing message and transform it to a more vibrant medium to promote your business.

Two of the most widely used networks are Facebook and LinkedIn, each offering distinctly different profiles and features.

Facebook is a free service that allows users to join networks organized by city, workplace, school, region, or area of interest, in order to connect with other people. You begin by creating a personal profile listing whatever kind of details you wish to include. Then you build a network by inviting and adding friends to whom you send messages and updates, which can also include work- and business-related activities. For business purposes, one of the most commonly used features is the Wall. Every user has one, and it's where people post their current status as well and announce upcoming events and anything of interest. The Wall is easy to update, so it makes for a very fluid, useful tool to broadcast special events and keep customers up to the minute about you and your enterprise.

LinkedIn, also free to join, positions itself as a professional online network designed to help professionals find and connect with one another. You start by building a profile, and since the site is tailored for business use, you create a résumé that summarizes your professional accomplishments, career goals, and areas of interests. The information you provide links you with colleagues, clients, partners, and potential customers, and you can look for jobs, post jobs, and list and find business opportunities. Think of it as an online Rolodex that has a huge global database. For the entrepreneur, it's a way to meet other people in the same field and learn more about the industry.

Blogging is another way to connect with your customer but in a much more informal way. A blog is a website centered on a theme. It can be a specific idea, something tangible, or something experiential like the person who blogs about the exact minutia of their day-to-day activities. There are hundreds of thousands of blogs, on everything imaginable, including the lifestyles of celebrity dogs, paper recycling, and stamp collecting. Name a topic and someone is passionately blogging about it. For business applications, blogging can serve several purposes.

- Blogs are a way to connect with other people in your industry. For example, a wine blogger could link his or her blog to others in the liquor industry or, if the focus is on red wines, link the page to the expert on sparkling drinks. It is a way to reach more potential customers and create a larger community outside of your specific industry.

- Blogs can also be a platform to convey information to your consumer. They're a place where you can give background and interesting historical details about your business and also serve up facts and frequently asked questions if someone was interested in learning more on the topic. And while you might use your website to convey content, a blog is typically a more personal, familiar forum that allows you to create a much more welcoming online presence. And unlike most websites, which have a more permanent construct, blogs are set up on very flexible platforms so that you can make changes easily and constantly update the content. Think of a blog as a newsletter or newspaper that has newsworthy headlines and current affairs that change frequently.

- Blogs can also give you a stage to shine on. By commenting on and contributing to other related blogs, you can position yourself as an industry expert. For example, as that red wine merchant, you can be a contributor on the "Fancy Food" blog and suggest wine pairing with their menus.

- Blogs can give immediate feedback. Most blogs invite reader comments, so potential customers can express what they like or don't like. It's a very dynamic and interactive way to evaluate your business and adjust your business offerings to give people want they want.

. . .

Finally, there's a form of social networking called Twittering. Twitter is a microblogging service that allows you to answer the question "What are you doing?" by sending short (140-character) text messages, called tweets, to friends and followers. Although it has a huge potential for narcissistic updates about someone's every twitch, for business Twitter can be used to broadcast your company's latest news or enable easy internal communication.

More social networking forms are bound to crop up in the future as Internet users find new ways to communicate and put stuff out into cyberspace, so be on the lookout for the next new thing.

Pauline Chan Lewis is an example of a socially responsible entrepreneur who proves that you don't have to sacrifice ethics for profits.

Pauline is the owner of oovoo design, an e-tail and wholesale company whose business is based on an alliance with a women's collective in Vietnam. She supports hundreds of women in Vietnam by selling their hand-embroidered handbags and carefully crafted works of art. She operates the strictly online business from her home. oovoo design represents a fulfilling career for her; for the working women and their families, it provides self-sufficiency, while women around the world enjoy the global crafts and uniquely designed handbags.

Pauline was born in Malaysia and as a young child moved frequently. She lived in the United States for two years, when her parents sought better job opportunities. The family lived in Hong Kong and Singapore, where Pauline was reared. She moved to New York to attend college and graduated with a degree in international relations. She wasn't certain what she wanted to do for work but always had an interest in bringing people together from different cultures. She married an American, and after working in international marketing research for ten years, she started to question her lifework and future. She felt she was putting her time and energy into something that had little meaning or self-fulfillment. She had taken some courses on how to start a business at the Virginia Women's Business Center, operating under the office of Small Business Development Centers, and this helped propel her into entrepreneurship. In 2004, she quit her corporate job with enough money from savings and investment for start-up business capital and living expenses for eighteen months.

Pauline began to research and connect to women in the United States and Southeast Asia who sold handcrafted items. After a trip to Vietnam, where she visited cooperatives and saw dozens of women making the handbags, she envisioned her future. She was impressed with the women's work ethic in very humble surroundings, and her mission became to translate her passion into a sustainable business with adequate sales and marketing. She would use the skills she had learned in the corporate world to apply to her own business. She developed a business plan and in 2004 did a soft launch with "bag parties" among friends and family and canvassing people on the street. After a year she ran out of friends and family, and returns were limited. She grossed $30,000, and even operating out of her home with her garage as the warehouse, and networking and marketing through her website, she was still not profitable.

She knew she needed another angle and decided to concentrate on the wholesale market. Over the next year she traveled to trade, gift, accessory, and fashion shows locally and nationally. This started to pay off, and she was able to outsource operations by using a fulfillment company to store and ship the bags. In December 2005, she was written up in Time *magazine, her business featured as a socially responsible company. That was the bump she needed, and the business exploded. She had found her hook in a unique product from a socially responsible company. The name oovoo evokes "ovo" for female, and the o's on either end represent the embroidery sewing circles of women working in groups of eight in their homes and joined by the cooperatives that handle the business.*

With wholesale representing 75 percent of the business, it was time to concentrate on the e-tail end and get the word out to individual consumers. Pauline upgraded the website, signed on with Facebook, started a blog, and began updating on Twitter to drive traffic to the site. Twitter, as mentioned before, is the social networking tool that allows you to connect with people and provide quick updates of your activity to a fan-club base, the people you have identified who want to follow what you are doing and connect to other people to expand your network. Pauline knows that she has to use every tool available to grow her Internet business. She also has sales representatives, but has noticed a decrease in orders from large retailers due to the economic downturn. Her main competition is from Cambodia, which, however, has a different style and product. Her target customers are mostly over forty and like bucking trends; they want to be comfortable but unique.

Pauline has received a Make Mine a Million award, and her sales have grown from $30,000 in 2004 to $500,000 in 2008. She expectss to be at her million by 2010 by expanding to include products of other socially responsible companies, and through concentrated e-tail marketing and targeted print advertising and public relations. She sees this as a way of generating media interest in the business and the women who make the bags. And from the looks of things, she's on track to make her million.

Pauline's business may be tied to an underdeveloped country, but her business is twenty-first century. She has created and grown it by using the most sophisticated Internet and e-commerce techniques. Through the use of social networking sites and a blog, she has built a recogniz-able presence with a fan base that follows her activities, and with the click of a mouse, she has spread the word and the sales potential.

EXERCISE 3 • Thinking about the nature of your business and which venues would be best suited for your product or service, list promotional methods you plan to use for your launch.

Design and create the content for a business card, flyer, brochure, or newsletter.

Depending on the function of your website, what information would you like to have on it? Is it for content and information only, or also for sales, processing payments, providing contacts, or scheduling appointments.

PROMOTION, THE INDIRECT APPROACH TO GETTING ATTENTION

Marketing includes all of the advertising strategies that cost money and also ways to promote your business that don't involve direct payment or associated cost. I define this as publicity and public relations. It is what you do and say about yourself and the business that creates interest and value in the minds of customers and the media. It's how you become newsworthy and generate buzz. It's not necessarily a single thing. Public relations is a combination of occurrences that result in positioning and branding. Your PR is made up of every single way you put your business out into the universe, from how you answer the phone to your customer service. It's about image and creating the best one possible, but to get media interest and press coverage you need to make your business newsworthy by coming up with a unique "hook." You do this through branding, which begins with selecting the name and logo to be placed in front of the customer. Think about the ultimate examples of branding where the brand name has actually become a substitute for the product, like Vaseline for petroleum jelly and Kleenex for facial tissues. Branding can add perceived value, so consider manufacturing opportunities to reinforce your tagline and sell your brand. When I set out to brand the business, the banner statement for the bookstore was that we were the largest bookstore in the country with the best inventory of books for African-Americans. I talked about the store as a beautiful place to shop, with sophisticated ambience, attentive customer service, and the finest events with well-known authors. Those taglines and the positive spin were repeated at all of our events and every other chance I got to talk about the business. Our customers believed and repeated the message. Of course we had to live up to the reputation, but that kept us challenged and pushed us to stay ahead of our competition. To establish your own brand, promote your business as being exclusive or unique and get others to repeat it.

To pump up your PR, consider joining a trade association and work to be recognized as an expert in the industry. Or teach a class at the university or give workshops on a specific area of expertise. Attract the spotlight by writing an article or critique and getting interviewed on TV or radio, or organizing a public service, such as a food drive, walkathon, or health fair, and participating in events that are covered by the local media. There are all kinds of creative projects that you can use to call attention to yourself and your business. Church functions and your social circles are also good places to spread the good word. Speaking of networking, don't forget to network, and network, and then network.

Patrice Clayton's business is the Harlem Tea Room, and to promote it, she has become the "tea lady."

Patrice knows exactly how she developed her love for tea. It was when she was a little girl, sitting with her grandparents, sipping tea, relaxing, and soaking up the company of her elders. When she grew up, she had an epiphany. She thought that Harlem would be an ideal place to open a tearoom. Tea salons were already a hot trend in downtown Manhattan, and it was her vision to create an elegant and relaxing place for residents to enjoy tea and socialize outside their homes in Harlem.

Patrice originally worked in corporate America in various marketing positions. After graduating from Case Western Reserve in Ohio with an MBA, she worked for American Express, where she developed business skills and the vision to become an entrepreneur. To explore her tearoom concept, she did a year of research, visiting libraries and tearooms. She learned about a tea tutorial from Tea: A Magazine. *The tea class, an intensive weekend course about the history, manufacturing, and distribution of tea, as well as managing tearooms, was offered twice a year on the East Coast. After completing the coursework, Patrice passed a written test and was awarded a certificate of expertise.*

Finding a location for her enterprise proved to be a difficult process, but she eventually obtained 2,000 square feet on Harlem's east side. Although the area didn't deliver heavy traffic, Patrice felt she could drive customers to her destination through marketing and branding. She had the idea that once she hung her sign, she'd be inundated with eager tea connoisseurs. The branding began with the name and production of a brochure, business cards, and a colorfully designed website. Then she created a space with a unique atmosphere, offering light food fare like soups, sandwiches, salads, and an assortment of desserts.

Although the media had anointed Harlem as an up-and-coming area, she knew marketing would be a challenge for this type of business. To get the word out, Patrice walked the walk and was a verbal advertisement and embodiment of her sophisticated product. Soft-spoken, well-mannered, and an expert in exotic teas, she talked about the business to everyone she met and networked at trade groups and local events. This word of mouth generated buzz and planted the seeds for her marketing strategy, primarily print ads. She launched with a press release, and the media jumped on the concept and promoted the business as another example of the exciting happenings in Harlem. The Tea Room was showcased on CBS, NBC, ABC, and the WB television network, and was featured in the Harlem News, The New York Times, Crain's, BusinessWeek, Savoy, Black Enterprise, Uptown, *and* O: The Oprah Magazine. *She received additional support from women's groups and women-owned businesses that used the Tea Room as a venue for hosting events, functions, and private celebrations. Patrice is active in her community and a participant in the Business Owners Ministry, and the pastor of her church has made several shout-outs. Whenever there is an article written about the chic side of Harlem, you can bet the Harlem Tea Room is mentioned.*

Despite the positive press and market penetration, the day-to-day business remained a challenge. With the addition of a point-of-sale system, Patrice learned that the heavier fare was her greatest revenue generator.

While Harlem was experiencing a renaissance, the customers still wanted more soul food–type items. She adjusted her menu to reflect this taste while keeping the tearoom concept.

Although Patrice had many of the right things going for her, like great branding and tons of positive press, it was not enough to sustain her business. After four years, she was forced to close. She couldn't overcome the lack of traffic in the area, the high rent, and the onerous terms of her lease. She will continue to do tea parties in homes and in locations selected by customers, and she looks forward to opening another tearoom that will benefit from the lessons she has learned.

Patrice put her business on the map by being engaged in her community and actively promoting her tea salon. She generated buzz by creating a unique enterprise and became the media darling and the recipient of loads of free publicity. These externally generated features brought more attention, cemented her status, and branded her business. Unfortunately, however, it wasn't enough, and the attention did not bring sufficient paying customers to her door. It's important to track the results and make sure the warmth of the spotlight translates into cold hard cash.

EXTRA EXTRA: ANNOUNCE YOUR NEW BUSINESS WITH A PRESS RELEASE

To put information in an easily digestible and concise form, write a press release that gives the launch information about your business, and a teaser about what exciting things are in store when people patronize your business.

A press release goes on company letterhead with the business name and location. The header should say "For immediate release" and list a contact person with a phone number. The body is double spaced, with a catchy header and succinct information. Remember, media gets tons of these so they will only take a quick look to determine interest and toss, unless it grabs their attention or it is a slow news day. Choose a medium where your business fits their "beat" or area of interest and you'll have a better chance for success. You can include a card or brochure to make a bigger impact. And release your news early in the day or week, when there is less pressure about deadlines and people aren't counting the minutes till quitting time. Make a list of media contacts that are favorably disposed to your business product or services. Keep your eyes peeled for a reporter's special interest and who is covering what and where. In the newspapers and magazines there are people who cover a specific beat, including writing and reporting on food, technology, restaurants, and even new interesting small businesses. As you listen to the radio and watch TV and cruise the Internet, you can hear and see segments and interviews that may potentially trigger coverage for your business. Yes, the Internet is an excellent way to send press releases.

The following is a sample press release.

HARLEM TEA ROOM
1793A Madison Avenue
New York, NY 10026

PRESS RELEASE

For Immediate Release
Contact:
Patrice Clayton
Phone: 212-348-3471
E-mail: info@harlemtearoom.com

Tea Room in Harlem

Welcome to Harlem, a little slice of heaven where guests of all ages are invited to partake of the relaxing ritual of "taking tea." This elegantly appointed oasis has a classic copper tea bar stocked with the largest selection and most flavorful blends of teas from around the world. Visitors can rest assured that the delectable tea accompaniments—exquisite desserts, tasty sandwiches, delicious salads, and hearty soups—are served in a warm, relaxed, and elegant environment.

Patrice Clayton, a Harlem resident and tea aficionada, has realized a dream to add this gem to the Upper East Side of Manhattan, located at 1793A Madison Avenue on the southeast corner of 118th Street.

On Saturdays from 1 to 4 p.m. guests of the Harlem Tea Room can enjoy a formal three-course afternoon tea, which includes fresh-baked scones, an assortment of tea sandwiches, and a sampling of desserts.

When allocating your marketing dollars, it's best to budget a larger amount in the beginning when your business is new and unknown. You may want to make a big splash and launch with a grand opening or kick-off party with food, drink, and celebrities. The goal is to generate interest and a feel-good experience about your business that will ultimately extend to your bottom line. It starts with the word of mouth—getting tongues wagging and having customers spread the positive vibe among friends and relatives that will come back in the form of sales. Marketing is an ongoing process that does not end. You will need to devise ways not only to get the customers in but also to keep them coming. Once the business is up and running, use observation and research skills to determine what works best. Stay in touch with your customers to determine what they like and dislike, and keep an eye on the competition. Don't be afraid to "borrow" ideas and expand on and rework them to make them better. Creativity is the name of the game, and you need to think outside the box. For the Hue-Man in Denver, I developed a program to donate used and bruised books to schools in Soweto, South Africa. It was amazing how I was able to solicit partners for the project and get an article written about it in *The New York Times*.

For Regina Brooks, Serendipity is a fitting name and description of her literary agency.

Marketing starts with the name of your business. It was serendipity when Regina started a so-ho (small-office, home-office) literary agency representing authors and managing their writing careers. She assists in writing book proposals, pitches the projects to publishers, and sells the works. She also negotiates contracts, is the liaison between the author and editor, and works postpublication to promote and market the book. Regina has approximately eighty clients in various stages of development, which is a credit to her business plan and excellent marketing strategies. Positive word of mouth is her best promotional tool and has allowed her to secure a position as an expert in the field. And it's that good buzz that's made her a sought-after speaker with engagements around the world at various writers' workshops, book conferences, and book fairs. Regina is supported by an excellent professional website that lists all of the necessary components for potential clients to evaluate her skills and capacity as an agent.

When Regina started out, she was headed in an entirely different direction, out to space, literally. With a degree in aerospace, she planned to continue her education and earn a Ph.D. in biomedical engineering to pursue the astronaut program. There was, however, another side to Regina, who wanted to take a more serious look at writing, so she joined an organization called Black Women in Publishing. Regina applied to the Howard University Publishing Program and after completing the course made a 180-degree career turn. A professor praised her writing and encouraged her to take a publishing job in sales as a stepping-stone into editing. She found a sales rep position at John Wiley & Sons, and within a year she became an editor. Regina moved to McGraw-Hill to work on computer books and while there got the idea to start her own business . . . and that idea stuck. Finally, in 2000, she decided to make her move, and with two clients and savings she quit her day job and started her literary business. To supplement the start-up, she leveraged her publishing relationships by offering freelance editorial services. As an agent, she receives 15 percent of the book deal, which includes the advance and royalties. Initially she lived from her savings but has built her client list and can now support herself and staff. Regina encompasses the three parts to being successful in her field. First, an agent needs to be a good writer. Second, one must have the ability to sell ideas and market projects. Third, it is important to be able to negotiate contracts as well as manage authors' careers. Regina learned all of these things in the book business, which she then packaged, marketing herself as an authority in a crowded and competitive field.

Regina worked to stand out in a tough industry. She positioned herself as an expert by initially volunteering her time to speak to groups of fledgling authors about the publishing industry, which gave her contacts and visibility. Thanks to a targeted marketing strategy, she has made herself an invaluable resource in the publishing business and the person people turn to for advice and expertise.

ENTICE YOUR AUDIENCE

The use of incentives is another way to promote your business on a shoestring budget. It draws attention and everyone likes a bargain. Before you open, you can stimulate interest with a discount, coupon, or free gift to encourage people to call or come through the door. After opening, your computer software can identify your best customers, to whom you can send a coupon that can be redeemed for merchandise, with a letter that identifies them as frequent buyers. You can also give rebates; for example, for every ten dollars they spend, you give customers a token worth a dollar in cash on their next purchase. The holiday season, when the amount spent per visit is at the highest, is a good time for this kind of promotion. Customers like coupons; it makes them feel good and like they're getting something for free. Don't expect a huge rate of return, however. Most retailers know the redemption rate is 30 percent to 50 percent. You can create all types of frequent buyer programs and invent opportunities for celebrations, which you can spice up with discounts, contests, games, and giveaways. Offering deep discounts on slow-moving items is another incentive. Also promote gift certificates, which allow customers to share the store experience with others, even if they don't know specifically what someone might want.

> **EXERCISE 4** • This exercise will require that you go beyond advertising and come up with creative ways to call attention to your business.
>
> Name at least three ways you can promote your business through PR.
>
> Name three local contacts for public relations.
>
> Can you brand your business? How will you reinforce the brand?
>
> Write a press release about your business, and list the distribution methods.
>
> List three ongoing marketing strategies, whether PR or advertising. How much will each cost?

In addition to becoming an entrepreneur, you have just become an advertising and public relations agency and created a marketing plan for your business. By completing the exercises listed in this chapter, you have identified your strategies to get and keep customers.

Chapter Nine

Step 9

Help Wanted: Hiring Employees

M e, myself, and I. That was essentially the staff when I opened my first store, and the hours kicked our collective butts. I would come in early to get ready for opening and then stay late after closing to do the paperwork that I could never seem to get done in between customers. I was doing what I loved, but it was exhausting and starting to suck the life out of me. I was tired of being tired. Although the business was growing, I had just started to pay myself so I was anxious about hiring someone else and not having enough money to sustain another salary. But I knew that if I continued like this, I'd fall over dead, so I decided to hire an employee. I put up a sign in the store and ran an ad in the neighborhood newspaper. My first employee was an actor who needed a flexible job more than a big salary. This worked for me because the retail book business doesn't pay big bucks. Hiring him freed me up to devote more time to business matters and marketing while my employee concentrated on sales, which he did very well. My subsequent employees were overqualified, but their lives were in transition, and they basically needed some short-term income to tide them over until they could get themselves together. They were all avid readers and gave great customer service, but I knew working at the bookstore was not part of their long-term career plan. They came from all kinds of employment backgrounds: social work, banking, public relations, and media. They were grateful to have a job in a bookstore while they worked on their next career move. It was a win-win situation; I nurtured them in their transition and they nurtured our customers. Some of our customers became our best employees, since they knew the business and understood what it took to turn casual shoppers into satisfied customers. As a community service I hired ex-offenders, but before they were offered a job, they had to volunteer at the store. Given the difficulty for ex-cons to find work, they were extremely loyal.

In Harlem there was a more formal hiring structure, since we were a larger operation and needed more employee coverage. We hired weekday staff and a separate weekend staff, using a mix of part- and full-time employees. At the beginning, salaries were minimum hourly wage, with the exception of the store manager, who was on salary. We gradually had to raise wages to compete with other retail operations.

One of my worst firings was of an employee who was taking money by coming into the store after hours. We discovered the cash loss and determined the culprit by tracking their keypad use at two a.m. Another employee had a drinking problem and was tardy. It was important to keep records, so I documented the effect on job performance, gave him a warning, and placed him on probation before eventually letting him go. I always tried to work with a troubled employee before firing, unless it was for something intolerable like stealing.

. . .

This chapter will move you from being a business owner to being someone's boss. You will learn how to determine if you need to hire employees, where to find them, and how to qualify them, plus how to plan for the additional considerations that come with employees, like payroll taxes and benefits, and will also give you the tools to manage and motivate your staff.

Initially, your entire staff roster may consist of you. As your business grows, you'll assess the workload and recognize the need to hire at least one other person. If you've never been in charge of hiring in your previous positions, this can be a daunting task. Finding good people is always a challenge. We start out wanting someone who can do everything and walks on water, but you may have to settle on someone who can just paddle a boat, or maybe just float.

To help navigate the staffing minefield, use the following as a guide to take you through the hiring process from start to finish. It provides the information you'll need and the questions to ask and answer for your business.

ASSESSING YOUR STAFFING NEEDS

- *Do you need to hire someone?* If from the start you knew there would be too much work and you would need to hire employees as in Hue-Man in Harlem, then hiring is not a question. The other scenario is the business is flourishing and you are working yourself to death, even staying up nights obsessing about all the things you have to do. If that's the case, you're actually losing business because you're too busy doing marketing or you're neglecting or ineffective in completing daily responsibilities, or both. You then have to determine how much your time is worth and if you are the best person to be doing all that work or if your time would be better spent focusing on other activities. Make a list of all the tasks that you do and objectively separate all of the tasks that someone else could do. This exercise will tell you if you need to hire someone full- or part-time, or perhaps get an intern.

- *Do you have the space?* If you have been working in the space by yourself, determine if there is enough room for someone else. Is there enough separation for you not to bump into each other and be a distraction? Can you convert the space and make it comfortable? This is a big factor if the business is home-based or in small office space. How will you adapt to being so up-close and personal with another person? How much will it cost to convert, and what equipment will you need to add, such as a desk, chair, or telephone?

- *Do you have the money?* How much can you pay? Will you be able to squeeze out enough money for your current expenses and add on a salary? Review the money situation to determine how much you have to spend. How much are you getting paid? What! Nothing? *Stop—pay yourself first!* Many new business owners do not pay themselves. It was three years before I took a salary; however, I recommend that you begin to pay yourself something at the beginning, even if it is small. You're working your fingers to the bone, and you need to be paid for all your hard work. It may seem a bit of a stretch, but the money will come and hopefully there will be a time when your salary matches your dedication.

- *Calculate the cost of a new hire.* Start with the salary based on an hourly or a flat wage; then add 15 percent to 20 percent, depending on benefits. There is a 12 percent out-of-pocket employee obligation that is paid to FICA, workers' compensation, and unemployment insurance. Anything above that can be an add–on, like paying a portion of health insurance. If the base salary is $3,000 a month, include a minimum expense of $330 per month. Then you'll determine if you'll offer sick leave, vacations, and personal time off. You may want to set aside a little in advance.

- *Calculate the amount of additional business* necessary to compensate for the expense, and compare that to the dollar figure you attribute to lost or untapped business.

- *Think about alternatives and options.* Would the hire be permanent or temporary? Would you be better off with a skilled independent contractor who is hired for a specific task or job, with a predetermined price and start and end dates? A wedding planner, for instance, hires someone specifically to do an event's flowers and decorations; you might hire an outside sales team to sell your product for a commission. Look at the salaries being paid by similar businesses within your industry to get an estimate. The salary can be a range or a specific amount in the beginning and increased later, depending on the applicants' education, skills, and performance.

After you've wrestled with the decision to hire an employee, you'll need a job description to be clear about what they'll be doing. To begin, keep it simple by writing a few sentences about the job duties and responsibilities. Next, identify the behavior and body of information necessary for the job. What skills and abilities are required?

You should consider the following qualifications and character traits when shopping for staff:

- Promptness and reliability, particularly if they'll be responsible for opening the doors (preferably on time).
- Honesty, always important but absolutely critical if your employees will handle money.
- Previous experience, and specifically in sales if you're in retail.
- Presentation and verbal skills.
- Credentials necessary that are specific to your business, like the required minimum education, experience, and certification.
- Any additional skills or special training pertaining to the work requirements.

EXERCISE 1 • Help wanted—or not.

This exercise will help you decide if you need an employee by reviewing what you currently do, what you need done, and if it would be impossible even for Wonder Woman to do the job. Use the information and answers to assess your staffing needs.

List tasks separated into those you must do and things someone else could handle.

Assess space and any conversion costs.

Calculate monetary cost of hiring someone.

> Factor in additional income needed to cover the cost. If you need an employee(s), complete a comprehensive job description with a salary.

FINDING EMPLOYEES

Now that you've decided to throw yourself a life preserver and hire someone, where do you look for employees? Sometimes the best place to start the search is in your own backyard. Spread the word through friends, acquaintances, and customers, and by networking with others in your industry. Then put out queries in places where you think you'd find the type of people you're looking for. If you're looking for students, post notices in common areas at colleges and universities. Or put up signs in local businesses, and visit programs that are preparing people for work situations. In my experience I found that ads in local newspapers yield big numbers and require a lot of sifting through. In your ad, you'll want to let people know how they can apply and ask them to send a résumé. Then you can pluck out the best to interview first. If you are looking for only one person, an informal search may be best and cheapest.

Out of necessity, Shannon Ayers Holden of Turning Heads Salon and Day Spa became an expert at staffing and all of the administrative responsibilities and emotional nuances that come with managing people.

Almost immediately after she took over Turning Heads, sales plummeted because of the departure of two of the salon's top stylists. Determined to succeed, Shannon dug in her heels and with concentrated effort got the business back on track. Shannon worked hard to stabilize her business. She became her own landlord by purchasing and renovating a space and moving and expanding her salon, but she still struggled with an unpredictable and at times a maddening variable that had jeopardized her business from the start . . . employees. From the high-maintenance divas who grace you with their fabulous presence to Miss Memory Loss who forgets everything you tell her, obtaining and retaining consistent, reliable, and skilled staff to provide quality services and excellent customer service is one of her greatest challenges. Through trial and error Shannon has become an expert in employee management and keeps the top-notch staff at Turning Heads on their toes. The ten-chair salon and day spa now has a 23,000-client database, an active website, and offers massage, facial, manicure and pedicure, waxing, body wraps and scrubs, and all types of hair services.

Shannon has created a structured hiring procedure. She requires that applicants must come to the job with some professional experience, be a team player, be honest, and have three professional references. All of the service providers (stylists, massage therapists, estheticians, and nail technicians) are required to be licensed in their skill set, do a practical demonstration to show their proficiency and, for stylists, have a portfolio. For administrative support, experience is needed in customer service, and cashier and phone work.

Most of all, what Shannon looks for or "feels" for is a sense of integrity and honesty. Her motto is that you can teach customer service skills and proper business etiquette, but you cannot teach integrity. You either have it or you don't. And she finds that it usually comes through during the interview.

. . .

The following is a job description for front desk coordinator/receptionist at Turning Heads Salon and Day Spa that Shannon placed in the newspaper and gave to people inquiring about the Help Wanted sign in her window.

Busy salon and spa in Upper Manhattan seeks coordinator/receptionist (full- or part-time) to be part of its front desk team.

Responsibilities include but are not limited to:

- Answering phones
- Booking appointments for staff
- Cashiering
- Retailing products
- Customer service. Being the first point of contact for clients.

Must have experience managing and answering busy phone system and coordinating schedules of many people. Proven track record in retailing, sales, and customer service preferred.

Necessary qualifications: Applicant should be a team player; have a positive attitude; be able to follow direction; and be able to take initiative and work independently.

Candidates under serious consideration will also need three professional references.

THE INTERVIEW

The candidates have been rounded up, and it's time to meet face-to-face with that bright shiny person from the résumé. Before you start the interview, you need to be clear about your goal, which is to determine the capacity and ability of that person to do the job. I start with a basic question of why they are applying for the position and what most interested them. All of the questions should be job related and not personal; there are all kinds of materials that say legally what you can and cannot ask. If this is your first time conducting an interview and you're unsure about the procedure, follow the job description and their résumé by asking about their work experience and qualifications. Then you can ask about their goals and how this job will help to fulfill them. And when in doubt, follow your gut, since you'll be working closely with this person and you want a good fit and a positive contributor, and not an employee from hell. Be prepared for questions and be honest about your expectations. After the interview call to check references to determine what other people and past employers think about your applicant. You cannot ask questions about race, color, sex, religion, age, disability, or marital/family status, and using this as a basis in your hiring criteria is considered discriminatory. If race is not obvious, you cannot inquire about their origin as a "back door" to get the information. Another potential pitfall is asking about someone's family status and if they are planning a family. An example would be if during an interview a potential employee mentions she is a newlywed. You cannot ask if she's planning on having children so you could avoid maternity leave, and you may not inquire of a woman with children about child care to determine if that will cause work interruption. If in doubt, don't ask!

YOU'RE HIRED

Once you've rated the applicants and decided on a winner, notify the person and get an acceptance. Also, make a courtesy call to interviewees to let them know you made a selection. Say something positive to make the medicine go down easier and defuse any negative feelings. Keep a résumé on file of the best "also ran" applicants in case of another opening. The next step is to make sure you're prepared for the first day. You should have an operations manual or even just a sheet about the way things are done at your business, which includes personal policies. It can also be a simple list of employee accountability and employer responsibility. These are the dos and don'ts that you absolutely need to have written and reviewed to ensure compliance, clarify expectations, and avoid misunderstandings down the road. A good idea with a new hire is to set up a probationary period, typically three to six months. It's like a motor vehicle lemon law, which lets you test-drive a car before actual purchase and return it if it's a clunker. Along with starting salary, you might also have planned increases after a prescribed amount of time or other financial or sales incentives. Then determine any benefits, like vacation, time off, and holidays. As you iron out the beginning, give some thought about the end and the requirement for giving notice to make sure you have time to find a replacement.

WHO'S THE BOSS?

It's official, your new hire has started work. Congratulations, you've just been promoted/demoted to supervisor/manager, and you need to have a plan for how you will work with your staff. First, look at your management style. Do you rate 10 on the bossy scale, or are you a wishy-washy one? Hopefully, you're somewhere in the middle and treat employees as you wish to be treated. Think about your best manager and how they enhanced your work experience.

Here are a few keys to being a good boss.

Orientation. No one likes to be thrown into a situation without guidance, so have a specific training plan to teach them the job.

Supervision. Give direction without being overbearing, and allow them latitude to be independent.

Constructive criticism. Keep expectations clear, and be direct when they're not being met or where there needs to be improvement.

Praise. I cannot stress enough the importance of giving praise, since it's easy to focus only on what's wrong and neglect to celebrate what is right.

Regular performance reviews. It is important to discuss how an employee is doing, both the positives and the negatives, and to provide a forum for employee feedback.

EXERCISE 2 • This exercise will examine your hiring process, if you followed a procedure or just went with the first warm body out of desperation.

What was your process: formal, informal, and do you create a template that you can duplicate?

> Why did you select the person you hired, and what are the person's qualifications?
> Create a list of policies and procedures. It can be a brief fact sheet if you prefer.

Along with staff comes salary and Uncle Sam, who has just become your other permanent new hire. Consider using a payroll service that keeps track of deductions and obligations for state, city, and federal taxes because the IRS will demand its money. This way you will know your financial obligations so you can set aside funds to pay taxes. A bookkeeper often handles this job.

Donna Walker-Kuhne of Walker International Communications Group shows that a carefully hired, well-trained staff is worth the time and money investment.

Donna started her business in 2002 with one employee. She hired an acquaintance, a member of her church, whom she knew was organized, reliable, and had office skills that were necessary in developing the business. Since then, Donna has grown and has four full-time and two part-time employees and several interns. She sees her business as a way to bridge the gap between the community and culture and works to identify groups with a critical mass of diverse members and introduce them to the arts. She partners with community organizations whose members come from all kinds of backgrounds, and she designs strategies, products, and events to promote group sales to a variety of venues and performances. One of her first projects was partnering with a service union and arranging for its many members to attend a performance of the Alvin Ailey Dance Company. Some of her other clients are the New York City Opera and Broadway theatrical productions like August Wilson's Radio Golf *and* Three Mo' Tenors.

Donna had an appreciation for the arts at an early age. When she was seven years old, her mother took her to a performance of the Bolshoi Ballet, which inspired her to study ballet. After meeting an African-American lawyer at a career fair, that dancer's vow of poverty went out the window and she set out to make some real money as an attorney. She graduated from Howard University Law School and continued to study dance as a hobby. In her spare time, Donna volunteered at a performing arts center across the street from the Family Court where she worked, and nine years later she crossed the street for good. She left the corporate world for nonprofit, where she remained for the next two decades. Donna worked primarily for the Dance Theatre of Harlem and the Public Theater in New York, developing skills in grant writing, administration, ticket sales, and audience development. She decided to start her own business, fulfilling her dream of entrepreneurship. Also motivated by maternity, Donna had recently adopted a baby and needed an income source and a flexible schedule.

Because of the nature of her business, Donna looks for employees with experience in the arts and marketing but will take eager applicants who have an interest in culture and can learn fast on the job. Donna hires based on the needs of her business and when she has a new client or project. She picks from a network of contacts and has never advertised for a position. Sometimes she knows someone she wants to hire and then creates a position based on the business need. Donna, like most small business owners, started by doing her own payroll, but after a year she decided to outsource those functions.

She hired Administaff, a professional employer organization serving as a full-service human resources department for small business. Administaff handles the payroll and structures employee benefit packages, which include vacation; health, life, and dental insurance; and 401(k) pension plan.

Donna understands the importance of maintaining good employee relations and relies on Administaff to put together the most optimal but cost-efficient plans. One of her employees once asked for a raise to pay for health insurance, which was over a hundred dollars per month for an individual, but by restructuring her benefits package, Donna was able to cover her employees for forty dollars per month and provide better benefits. She knows how she felt as an employee and remembers and appreciates employers who cared about her overall long-term well-being and tries to create a nurturing type of environment at her business. Donna is currently working with Administaff to develop job descriptions, annual performance appraisals, and an employee manual. She recognizes that her previous way of managing employees was nontraditional and less structured, but with the current staffing, she is reevaluating her method and wants to make it a more professional and standardized procedure. Donna figures that it takes a year to bring a staff member up to speed, so the cost of the services is well worth the expense, since better polices improve employee retention, which saves her in hiring and retraining costs.

Donna's business is structured as a Subchapter S Corporation, which provided the tax advantage for a start-up that will not necessarily make a profit but can support itself and give Donna a salary. It's a home-based business, located in the family's Victorian house, which had previously housed a physician's home/office. After five years, she has more than doubled her original revenues and expects to increase by 10 percent annually. Donna positions herself as an industry expert by teaching at New York University, Brooklyn College, and Columbia University. She has written a book, Invitation to the Party: Building Bridges to the Arts, Culture and Community, *in response to people asking how she does what she does. This forced Donna to develop a template for replication, and eventually she would like to create similar businesses in other major cities. As her business has grown, Donna made a conscious decision to reinvest money in consulting services and employee benefits. Donna needs to be able to delegate to a competent staff, and her next hire will be an office manager/personal assistant who will handle her speaking schedule and individual activities and free her up from staff and clerical functions. This will allow her to concentrate on marketing and making connections that will grow her business.*

Donna recognized early on that for her, the benefits of outsourcing payroll and other human resources functions greatly outweighed the costs. She also places a high value on employee satisfaction and strives to create a supportive and rewarding work environment for her staff.

YOU'RE FIRED!

Things started out great with your eager new employee, and then you hit a bump in the road. It becomes apparent that you and the employee will need to part ways. It may be that they are not doing the job, have unacceptable behaviors, or are creating some kind of stress in the workplace and on the business. First, step back, take a breath, pull out the job description as a guide, and identify what they are doing or not doing that is job related. Understandably, you want to avoid going through the process of finding a replacement, but you can't afford to jeopardize the business and cause a negative impact on other employees by keeping this person around. As you prepare to meet with the employee, have a plan and know what you want to say. Give specific, dated job-related and job-performance examples and document when and how many times the problems occurred. For example, how often they were late or called in unable to come to work; what job responsibility was not fulfilled; any inappropriate behavior or responses to coworkers or customers or insubordination with managers. You should give the person a time frame for improvement, and the next step would be probation or termination. If termination is imminent, as when someone is stealing or there's another serious business transgression, the employee should be let go immediately because such an employee can be disruptive and vindictive or crazy. If at a later time you are asked to give a reference for a terminated employee, rather than go into ugly details about the firing, it is best to say you would not rehire.

Human resources covers such a wide variety of issues, like hiring, firing, managing, training, wages, and procedures, with some having legal compliance and regulation implications, that it may be helpful to read or go online to familiarize yourself with related information. The last thing you want to happen is for an employee to have a complaint that results in a court proceeding. You want to establish safety rules, progressive discipline that gives employees opportunity for correction, and clear guidelines for consequences. Mary Holihan's book on the subject, *365 Answers About Human Resources for the Small Business Owner: What Every Manager Needs to Know About Work Place Law*, is concise and easy to understand and will help you avoid mistakes, possibly legal ones.

You're in the homestretch of mapping out your enterprise. You've found the final piece to the puzzle and are ready to add "live bodies" to support all your hard work and lighten your load.

Chapter Ten

Step 10

Ready, Set, Stop!
Write Your Business Plan,
Then Go!

Whenever I am on a panel, the moderator always asks at the end: "What one thing can you say to be most helpful to other entrepreneurs?" My answer is always the same: Do a business plan. It's the same whenever I give my talk about the steps to entrepreneurship, and I'm amazed at how many people interested in starting a business have not written a business plan. I typically conduct my workshops through the small-business department at banks, so attendees are presumably getting close to the money stage and are looking at the bank as a possible source of funds. These budding entrepreneurs are ready to move full speed ahead by borrowing money, renting space, and buying equipment, but they can't answer fundamental questions about breakdown of expenses, cost of product, or number of units necessary to be profitable. Often it is difficult for them to even clearly describe their concept; it's more like "I'm gonna open a lounge, serve drinks, maybe have some food." What?

And with this vague scheme they are on the verge of signing on the dotted line for a loan or to secure a lease. I have to give them a reality check and basically tell them to "back up . . . slow your roll." I encourage them not to jump in with blind enthusiasm but rather to tackle the hard thing first and write a business plan, since the success of their business might very well depend on it.

This chapter will explain what a business plan is and how it serves as the foundation of your enterprise. This step will show you the benefits of writing a business plan and the consequences if you don't. It will demystify the process and provide you with a format and table of contents so that you can break it down into manageable pieces.

WRITING A BUSINESS PLAN

Hopefully, this book has answered many questions and motivated you to take the next steps and write your business plan. This is your road map, which will seal your commitment, keeping you focused on where you want to go and on track and actively working to get there. This was my motivation for writing the book this particular way. Writing a business plan can seem like an overwhelming task, and I wanted to break down the steps into digestible chunks. How do you eat an elephant? One bite at a time. I want you to overcome your fear and recognize how much you know, and what you don't know, and then make it your mission to find the answers. Planning for any venture is important, and this is probably one of the biggest undertakings you'll attempt in your lifetime. So put the work into the front end to generate a positive outcome on the back end.

It is your time and money, so invest wisely in you. By doing the exercises in each chapter, you already have the basics for a business plan. We will walk through the business plan and the chapters to demonstrate that you already have the foundation based on your answers.

WHAT IS A BUSINESS PLAN?

Like a résumé of your business, the plan speaks to who you are, what you intend to do, and how you are going to do it. The following is a list of reasons why you need a business plan:

- It takes your idea out of your head and makes you birth it to paper.
- It forces you to focus, crystallize your idea, and create something you can touch and feel just like your business.
- It takes it out of wishing and fantasyland, and moves you toward a reality.
- You can begin to organize around your goal to determine what you need, what you have, and how you make up any difference.
- It is a tangible way to introduce your business to others who may want to be a part of your venture.
- You will develop action steps that are concrete, and will do things with regularity and have a timeline for completion.
- It says to you and to others that you are serious and committed to your concept.
- It is a device for tracking the progress of your business, and a simple method to determine if you are on point with your business goals.

- It is an instrument that allows you to make adjustments if necessary, as things do not always go according to plan and you may need to make changes midstream.
- It is a mechanism for planning for the future by providing a starting point to determine where you would like to see your business years down the road.
- It is a document for potential investors and helps the banker to qualify you for a loan. When you are asking for money, they want something in writing.

From the above, you can see that a business plan is essential and necessary if you are really serious about business. The amount of information and specificity will vary depending on the audience. For example, investors and bankers will require more detail and will be most interested in the financial analysis. The nature and the size of your business is also a factor in the content and detail of your plan. If your business is a home-based, sole proprietorship that is self-funded and service based, you may need just a few chapters and less detail, as the plan is basically for you to chart your development rather than for investors whom you want to convince of your capacity and ability to sustain the business.

Here is an example of a Table of Contents for your business plan:

1. Executive summary
2. Business description product/service
3. Industry overview
4. Operation?
5. Owners/principals
6. Location
7. Market data/competition

8. Marketing strategies
9. Management and personnel
10. Financial summary

Below are the main components of a business plan:

Cover Sheet

This contains the name, address, and telephone number of the business, using your letterhead with your logo to give some visual interest. It states who prepared the business plan and the date. If the plan is to be distributed, each one is numbered and you keep track of distribution.

Table of Contents

This portion lists the contents of the plan to help the reader navigate the information in an orderly manner. It is a preview to the detail the plan contains (see sample above).

Executive Summary

This is a one-page summary that is a snapshot of the business. It describes the business idea, location, capacity of the owners and principals, and market and financial highlights. This can be written after you have completed your business plan. The information should be concise and touch on key points of the plan.

Organizational Plan

This will be your main section, with the most chapters.

- *Business description product/service:* It explains what you plan to deliver and why it is necessary, based on a needs assessment, which is a brief description of why you think people will want to buy your products or services. This information is in Chapter Two, Exercise 1. You will want to be as detailed as possible in your description. Assume that the reader is not familiar with the product or service; your job is to make certain they fully understand what you want to do.

- *Industry overview:* What is happening in the industry and how will it affect the business? What is the industry history and what are current and future trends? This information is contained in Chapter Two and your response to Exercise 2.

- *Operations:* The description of planned operation, which is the way you will operate the business, is basically the nuts and bolts of what you will do and how you will do it. The amount of detail depends on whether you are in retail, manufacturing, sales, or service. This information is in Chapter Two.

- *Information on the owners and principals:* Who are the people starting and operating the business, their background, capacity, résumé, credentials, and track record? Describe the various roles and responsibilities of others involved, as discussed in Chapter Four, Exercise 2. While you are primarily describing yourself as the owner, you will include any key persons involved in the day-to-day business activity. The narrative can come from your cover letter that you were asked to compose in Chapter One, Exercise 1, which will include a description of who you are and what experience and skill sets you have that qualify you to deliver the services. What special training is necessary and what do you possess? Additional material for this section is contained in Chapter One, which is gathered from the list of characteristics for entrepreneurs. This is where you praise and promote yourself and the passion comes through.

- *Location of the business:* Where are you putting your business? What is the physical structure and square footage? This information is found in Chapter Six, Exercises 1 and 2 for Home-based. It includes the details of the proposed tenancy arrangements found in your leasing contract and how you will prepare the space for occupancy, for example, any additional landlord and tenant finishing. This is found in Chapter Six, Exercise 4. You will also list projections and a timetable for completion, as found in Chapter Six, Exercise 3.

- *Equipment:* You will need special equipment to operate your business, including computers and industry-specific hardware that enhance operations and productivity. You have described the equipment in your start-up costs in Chapter Five, Exercise 1.

- *Business structure:* The type of legal structure you plan to use to launch your business is covered in Chapter Four.

- *Personnel information:* Whom do you plan to hire to assist in your business and how will you manage them? This is contained in Chapter Nine and the responses to Exercises 1 and 2.

Marketing Plan

- *Market data and analysis/competition assessment:* Who are your customers, what is the size of your market, and where are they purchasing the products and services? This is discussed in Chapter Seven. Once you have described your competition, how will you challenge them? This information is contained in Chapter Three, Exercises 1, 2, and 3.

- *Marketing strategies:* How you will locate your customers, get the word out, and what you will do to keep them coming back to do business with you are all discussed in Chapter Eight, Exercises 1, 2, 3, and 4.

Financial Information

- *Income and expense projections:* What will it cost to start your business and what are the anticipated revenues and cash flow projections? See Chapter Five, Exercise 2. What is the source of the funding, capitalization, and how will the business handle debt service? Turn to Chapter Five, Exercises 3 and 4.
- Your accountant should prepare financial statements and cash flow statements.

Supporting Documents

This section contains documents necessary to support information and statements in the plan. Examples are résumés, articles of incorporation, lease agreements, and trademarks.

Go ahead, exhale! As you can see, there is no quick way to write a business plan, but once you have gone through the table of contents and fleshed out the parts, you've created a working draft. As you review your document, you may see areas that need refinement, but most of the hard work has already been done.

There are also books and software tools for business plan development that I urge you to review in bookstores and libraries. You can go online and search "How to Write a Business Plan," and you'll get "pay-for" products but also lots of free services. The best free options are Business Plan Pro, which gives you actual plans for different types of businesses, and Small Business Administration (SBA), which has a format for business plan development. Face-to-face contact with a consultant or workshops are available at SBA and your state's SBDC (Office of Small Business Development Centers). There are locations in cities around the country, which you can access by putting in your zip code or state.

As with anything in life, even if you have a plan and you're prepared, things change, stuff happens, and you make headway through a series of trials and errors. This is particularly true with businesses because you are often in untested waters. What happens when something goes wrong?

Melanie McEvoy, founder of McEvoy & Associates, has experienced a mixed bag of starts and stops and experimented with several different business forms, partners, and sources of income until she found a good fit.

Melanie is a perky, bright woman with just the right personality for her work as a fund-raiser and event planner for issue-oriented nonprofit companies. She creates a strategic plan and does everything from addressing invitations to arranging centerpieces to maximizing event revenue. Melanie is passionate about her beliefs but also a savvy money manager, making her a tough negotiator when dealing with a variety of vendors and contractors. And she is extremely well organized and had excellent skills in managing multiple revenue streams and expenses.

Melanie developed her activist spirit during college in an unlikely place:

her hometown of Las Vegas. After the sting of the Webster *decision by the Supreme Court, which crippled* Roe v. Wade, *she became committed to maintaining abortion rights. When she graduated college, she moved to Washington, D.C., to be closer to the political action and at twenty-five became one of the oldest interns on Capitol Hill. She partnered with a consulting firm in D.C. that sent her around the country to work on political campaigns devoted to women's issues, and worked on political strategy, community organizing, fund-raising, and event planning. After a two-year stint of back-to-back political campaigns in New York, she began receiving calls from female candidates who wanted to hire her. The entrepreneurial wheels started turning, and she decided to open a fund-raising consulting business. This proved to be premature, since she didn't have a client base to support her business, so she struggled. To keep from going under, Melanie took a job with a colleague who had recently moved from home-based to an office and needed to hire an employee. They eventually merged their business into a partnership, and after four years Melanie bought her out for $30,000, paid over two years.*

In 2002, Melanie restructured the business as a sole proprietorship and focused on fund–raising for the nonprofit sector—a move that made her painfully aware of her own professional limitations. Her partners' skills were contract negotiating and managing the clients' expectations, while Melanie was excellent at handling the money and organization. Minus her partner, the business suffered a big decrease in revenue. She panicked and overcompensated by bringing in senior-level hires as well as full- and part-time assistants. This shock to the system was not the solution, and it forced Melanie to step back and reevaluate her plan. She relocated the office for the third time, downsized, and was able to increase and manage her client base. Restructuring gave her new traction, and from 2004 to 2006 she doubled her net revenue to $109,000; in 2007 revenue was $395,000.

McEvoy & Associates, which serves about a dozen clients a year, has two *full-time staff, consultants, independent contractors for projects, and part-time interns. When submitting a proposal, the client pays directly to outside vendors, including floral, catering, photography, design, and printing services. The business fee is based on the number of staff involved in the planning and execution, multiplied by an hourly rate. Initially, Melanie relied on her gut to determine fees, but she has honed pricing to an exact science. There's little margin for error, since this is her direct source of income and wrong calculations go directly to the bottom line. The fees are itemized and there's an initial retainer and monthly billings to manage cash flow. The work is seasonal, with the heaviest times in spring and fall. This puts pressure on the finances because she has staff and an office to maintain, so to cover her fixed costs she secured a $50,000 line of credit. The bank extended such a generous amount thanks to her long-term relationship with the lender and Melanie submitting two years of tax filings showing consistent income. She will access about $20,000 of her line at the beginning of the year, when business is slower, and will pay it down within three to four months after completion of the projects.*

Melanie plans to continue to grow her business by stepping up her marketing, updating the logo and website, and creating an e-newsletter and interactive blog. She's also recently initiated a strategic alliance with a home-based entrepreneur in Harlem who runs an event-planning business. Working with a skilled person will relieve Melanie from some of the day-to-day pressures and allow her to concentrate on new business development. And she'll be giving a helping hand to another up-and-coming entrepreneur as someone did for her.

Melanie's story demonstrates common mistakes and missteps and can serve as a cautionary tale for people thinking about starting their own business.

Here are some lessons to be learned from Melanie:

Look and plan before you leap. Before you decide to take the entrepreneurial plunge, you need to have a steady, identifiable (paying) client base.

Keep it simple, stupid. Don't overcomplicate things. When something doesn't go exactly as planned, and it seldom does, don't overreact or overcorrect.

There's no place like home . . . maybe. Depending on the nature of your business and living situation, try home-based, if possible, at least to start.

Take advantage of opportunities. Look for ways to establish relationships and partnerships with others so that it's a win-win for both.

Know your own worth. Don't undervalue yourself or your product or service by undercharging or giving it away. And in order for you to confidently sell it to your customers, you need to be sold first.

Being a techno geek is a good thing. By utilizing technology you can more easily manage expenses and revenues and build a "better, stronger, faster" marketing and promotion plan with online presence. Knowing how to do at least part of the technology piece yourself keeps money in your pocket.

Don't (always) be superwoman. You have to learn to delegate and also recognize that there are certain things that you're not that good at. Evaluate your strengths and compensate for the weaknesses.

It's okay to make mistakes. And you will. Just don't bang your head against the wall once and then do it over and over again (the wall is hard, your head is soft). Learn from your mistakes and don't repeat them.

Be patient and forgiving. When things take a wrong turn, pick yourself up, brush yourself off, and start again with new information and renewed confidence.

Finally, *Celebrate your successes.* You've worked hard and deserve that praise and positive feedback.

For your final exercise, after reading this book, I want you to jump-start your business.

You have a business idea; now you need to do three things to move it forward. For example, flesh out your idea, identify three competitors, complete a résumé to determine your qualifications, find three potential locations, subscribe to a publication about your industry, and sign up to attend a small-business workshop.

Do one of them this month and put a timeline on the other two.

Once you have completed three steps, do them more thoroughly, like filling in more comprehensive details about your idea or researching the products or services of your competitors and their prices.

Keep the forward momentum going by doing more things on your list.

Then get ready to write your business plan. Identify the steps you need to take and the information you need to gather. Set a time frame, and using the sample, complete the exercises that will generate the components of your plan.

Now you're ready. Put this book down and *get down to business.*

AFTERWORD

Once I completed the ten steps, I realized that it was really the jumping-off point into entrepreneurship and that there were still cycles of business that would occur as the enterprise developed and evolved. In this Afterword I want to leave you with some final pieces of information about the long-term future of your business and what I experienced as my stores matured.

After getting Hue-Man Bookstore in Denver up and running, we had three critical stages:

1. *Expansion of the store.* At the end of our third year in business, sales were growing at a rate of 15 percent annually, and I could foresee the need for additional space. The bookstore was located in a two-story attached row house occupying one of the four 1,500-square-foot units. The building had previously been used for

residences, although the zoning had been updated to include commercial use. On the first floor of each unit was a living room, dining area, and kitchen with three bedrooms and a bathroom on the second floor. The main portion of the store was in the living and dining rooms, and we used the kitchen for shipping and receiving. Upstairs was an office, and we displayed books for children and youth in the three bedroom spaces. The landlord offered the unit next to ours, which doubled our space and doubled our rent, and he agreed to knock out the walls to connect the units. After renovation, we were strapped for cash and barely able to handle the increased rent much less purchase additional inventory, but I had to trust the process and hope that in the long run it was the right thing to do. It turned out to be a good decision, since expanding the upstairs space gave us more seating space for author signing, which greatly increased revenue and boosted our claim as the largest African-American bookstore in the country. We significantly increased our traffic by hosting three to five author signings a week, as well as hosting community events. We received more media attention, and the community viewed the store as a destination and a place to rub shoulders with well-known authors.

2. *Purchase the building.* We successfully did a capital call to our customers with a personal letter inviting them to become shareholders in order to raise money for the down payment on purchasing the building. With five years of financial statements and documentation that showed that we could afford the mortgage payment, and some serious negotiations on the selling price, we closed the deal. Although our monthly payment was slightly higher than our rent, we now had tenant revenue and our tenants sold complementary African-American products.

3. *Succession planning.* When I was ready to retire the first time, my children were adults and living in New York. They had not grown up in the business and had no interest in managing or owning the store, so I chose to sell. Coincidentally, when I had made the decision, I met a business broker in New Orleans who had assisted in the selling of a bookstore and was moving to Denver. I took that as a sign and worked with him to develop a prospectus. It took two years and dozens of tire kickers to finally sell the business. When the idea of retirement resurfaced, I was at the Hue-Man in Harlem. I was ready to move on, so the partners and I decided to add a managing partner to replace me in the store. To prepare for the transition, she worked in the bookstore a year before my retirement in July 2004.

Perhaps the most critical stage of business occurs with growth and management of expansion. The growth of your business can occur from your current customers or come from new market penetration. It is every entrepreneur's expectation that their business will grow and even take off like a rocket, but unless Oprah anoints you as one of her "favorite things," you probably won't get to live out that fantasy. But growth does come, whether gradually or in a big spurt, and you will need to be prepared and have the management of the business under control. The kind of growth I'm referring to has significant impact on your business and requires that you make major changes.

The entrepreneur in the mature business has moved out of the survival mode and is no longer the single engine that keeps everything running. As you grow, you'll need to hire more employees, delegate responsibilities to others, and, in general, get more people involved. This is the time to think about how to extricate yourself and work on the business and not in it. You will develop people and systems to keep the business running without your direct input. You become the leader and thinker and begin to cut the apron strings. You'll learn to let go and let the business grow up.

Some of the considerations for mature business owners are:

- What is the origin of the growth? Has the business taken off by virtue of your tapping into a big unmet need? For example, you've opened a small print shop but had no idea of the size of the market and that people had been traveling a great distance to take care of their printing and copying needs. Now those needs can be satisfied closer to home.
- Is the growth seasonal as it is for retail, with the jump in sales at Christmas, Mother's Day, or Valentine's Day?
- Have you added new products? You developed a new line that complements your original business and is in great demand. As in your print shop, maybe you've added graphic design services, Internet access, and office supplies.
- Have you acquired a new arm to your business? Who knows, it may be your competition.
- You purchase property and become a landlord and generate rental income.
- Have you used a new strategy for increased market penetration or entered a new market? For example, at your print shop you've obtained the printing business of five churches in your area for weekly programs, prayer cards, and obituaries.

The above list can help you to determine the sustainability of your growth. With this growth, you need to revisit your business plan and begin to identify new space requirements, timely acquisition of more products, and the need to negotiate with your vendors for distribution. Consider if these changes will result in different promotion, pricing, resources, and infrastructure.

Staying in touch with your banker will pay off in this stage since you may need capital for acquisitions and expansion. You must be able to demonstrate that you are a good business risk, and have a good relationship, accurate records, and solid financials. Then you'll be in a good position to apply for a loan, line of credit, or additional funds on your current loans.

As a mature entrepreneur, you'll begin to look at various aspects of the business, taking one at a time to determine what you are doing, why you are doing it, and how well you are doing it. This requires examining your infrastructure to dissect the different parts of the business that require changing. An example is what is occurring with your inventory. Now you will need more of it, and will it have to be housed, so will you need storage space? And you may need a line of credit as expenses will go up and need to be paid before the revenue shows up on the books. Your staff may need to be increased, along with an increase in your hours and days of operation.

As you establish your business, you'll want to strengthen your branding. You might develop a design for a gift certificate with your logo, establish policies around the selling and redemption, and train staff how to handle the transaction. Branding extends to the smiling faces that work for your business. That means creating a more professional appearance of your staff with a uniform or dress code and training in customer service. Basically you begin to orchestrate consistency and predictability.

As you work on your business, you may consider new superheroes.

A *financial planner* can assist with setting up a benefits package, not only for yourself but also for your employees. They can help you develop a more sophisticated insurance coverage based on the business needs, which is essential if you have purchased property and have tenants. You can develop a retirement package by contributing money into a 401(k) account. A financial planner can explore investments to generate additional revenue and develop strategies for long-term wealth creation because a business is an investment and has value, particularly if you have property ownership options.

A *business coach* can consult about the overall business development to ensure long-term sustainability. They bring a trained pair of eyes to examine your business components and evaluate your infrastructure. It's also someone who can advise and counsel regarding the day-to-day decisions for business development. Just as you have a personal therapist for your individual problems, the business coach is there for your business issues and is someone whom you can confide in and who understands the business experience.

Your successor will be the new (less tired) you, and it's important to have a succession plan to determine who will succeed you if something happens to you or when you decide to leave the business or retire. You may have a family member or person with the interest and the capacity to step in to fill your shoes; if not, you might consider your business family employees. Employees know the business, and it can be a great opportunity to continue the legacy with someone who knows and is invested in the business. If there is no one in the wings and you want to sell the business, enter the accountant, lawyer, and business broker who will work to establish an actual price for the business, the name and logo, including the intangibles such as the goodwill.

It's important that your superheroes are with you throughout the process, from creating a prospectus to consummating the sale. Hopefully, you have developed a business that has created wealth for you, and when the time comes for you to leave, you can happily pass the torch to a worthy successor.

APPENDIX

Exhibit 1. Blank Schedules for Start-up Costs and Capital Budget

Start-up Costs	MONTH 1	2	3	4	5	6	7	8	9	10	11	12	TOTAL
Occupancy Deposit	$0	$0	$0	$0	$0	$0	$0	$0	$0	$0	$0	$0	$0
Telephone Deposit	$0	$0	$0	$0	$0	$0	$0	$0	$0	$0	$0	$0	$0
Utilities Deposit	$0	$0	$0	$0	$0	$0	$0	$0	$0	$0	$0	$0	$0
Legal and consulting/ Start-up	$0	$0	$0	$0	$0	$0	$0	$0	$0	$0	$0	$0	$0
Grand Opening/ Initial Campaign	$0	$0	$0	$0	$0	$0	$0	$0	$0	$0	$0	$0	$0
Total Start-up Costs [To Sales Line on Statement of Cash Flows]	$0	$0	$0	$0	$0	$0	$0	$0	$0	$0	$0	$0	$0

Capital Budget	MONTH 1	2	3	4	5	6	7	8	9	10	11	12	TOTAL
Equipment	$0	$0	$0	$0	$0	$0	$0	$0	$0	$0	$0	$0	$0
Furniture	$0	$0	$0	$0	$0	$0	$0	$0	$0	$0	$0	$0	$0
Signage	$0	$0	$0	$0	$0	$0	$0	$0	$0	$0	$0	$0	$0
Total Capital Expenditures [To Fixtures & Equipment on Statement of Cash Flows]	$0	$0	$0	$0	$0	$0	$0	$0	$0	$0	$0	$0	$0

Exhibit 2. Example of a Completed Cash Flow Statement

Company Name					
Pro Forma Statement of Cash Flows Year 1					
Beginning Cash Balance	$0	−$250	−$218	$4,785	$2,735
MONTH	1	2	3	4	5
Inflows from Operations					
Sales [Units Sold & Gross Revenue]			$2,000	$3,000	$4,000
Total Cash Inflows from Operations	$0	$0	$2,000	$3,000	$4,000
Inflows from Financing					
Equity Financing	$10,000				
Line of Credit $25,000	$9,000	$4,000	$7,000		
Total Cash Inflows from Financing	$19,000	$4,000	$7,000	$0	$0
TOTAL CASH INFLOWS	$19,000	$4,000	$9,000	$3,000	$4,000
Outflows from Operations					
Advertising & Promotion					
Car and Truck	$100	$100	$100	$100	$100
Insurance	$1,000				
Interest Payments		$68	$98	$150	$143
Legal and Professional	$250	$250	$250	$250	$250
Office Expense	$1,000	$100	$100	$100	$100
Rent	$1,000	$1,000	$1,000	$1,000	$1,000
Supplies	$600	$150	$150	$150	$150
Travel and Entertainment					
Telephone & Utilities	$200	$200	$200	$200	$200
Wages		$2,000	$2,000	$2,000	$2,000
Other Expenses	$100	$100	$100	$100	$100
Total Outflows from Operations	$4,250	$3,968	$3,998	$4,050	$4,043
Outflows from Financing					
Loan Payments				$1,000	$1,000
Total Outflows from Financing	$4,250	$3,968	$3,998	$5,050	$5,043
Outflows from Nonrecurring Expenses					
Fixtures & Equipment [Capital Budget]	$10,000				
Start-up Costs [Schedule of Start-up Costs]	$5,000				
Total Nonrecurring Expenses	$15,000	$0	$0	$0	$0
TOTAL OUTFLOWS	$19,250	$3,968	$3,998	$5,050	$5,043
TOTAL INFLOWS	$19,000	$4,000	$9,000	$3,000	$4,000
TOTAL OUTFLOWS	$19,250	$3,968	$3,998	$5,050	$5,043
NET CASH FLOWS	−$250	$33	$5,003	−$2,050	−$1,043
Ending Cash Balance	−$250	−$218	$4,785	$2,735	$1,693
Assumptions: See attached					
Loan Balance	$9,000	$13,000	$20,000	$19,000	$18,000
Interest Rate	9.000%	0.750%	0.750%	0.750%	0.750%
		$68	$98	$150	$143

	6	7	8	9	10	11	12	TOTAL
	$1,693	$1,658	$2,630	$3,610	$4,605	$5,615	$7,648	
	$5,000	$6,000	$7,000	$7,000	$8,000	$9,000	$10,000	$61,000
	$5,000	$6,000	$7,000	$7,000	$8,000	$9,000	$10,000	$61,000
								$10,000
								$20,000
	$0	$0	$0	$0	$0	$0	$0	$30,000
	$5,000	$6,000	$7,000	$7,000	$8,000	$9,000	$10,000	$91,000
								$0
	$100	$100	$100	$100	$100	$100	$100	$1,200
								$1,000
	$135	$128	$120	$105	$90	$68	$45	$1,148
	$250	$250	$250	$250	$250	$250	$250	$3,000
	$100	$100	$100	$100	$100	$100	$100	$2,100
	$1,000	$1,000	$1,000	$1,000	$1,000	$1,000	$1,000	$12,000
	$150	$150	$150	$150	$150	$150	$150	$2,250
								$0
	$200	$200	$200	$200	$200	$200	$200	$2,400
	$2,000	$2,000	$2,000	$2,000	$2,000	$2,000	$2,000	$22,000
	$100	$100	$100	$100	$100	$100	$100	$1,200
	$4,035	$4,028	$4,020	$4,005	$3,990	$3,968	$3,945	$48,298
	$1,000	$1,000	$2,000	$2,000	$3,000	$3,000	$6,000	$20,000
	$5,035	$5,028	$6,020	$6,005	$6,990	$6,968	$9,945	$68,298
								$10,000
								$5,000
	$0	$0	$0	$0	$0	$0	$0	$15,000
	$5,035	$5,028	$6,020	$6,005	$6,990	$6,968	$9,945	$83,298
	$5,000	$6,000	$7,000	$7,000	$8,000	$9,000	$10,000	$91,000
	$5,035	$5,028	$6,020	$6,005	$6,990	$6,968	$9,945	$83,298
	-$35	$973	$980	$995	$1,010	$2,033	$55	$7,703
	$1,658	$2,630	$3,610	$4,605	$5,615	$7,648	$7,703	
	$17,000	$16,000	$14,000	$12,000	$9,000	$6,000	$0	
	0.750%	0.750%	0.750%	0.750%	0.750%	0.750%	0.750%	
	$135	$128	$120	$105	$90	$68	$45	

Appendix

Exhibit 3. Example of Schedule of Units Sold and Gross Revenue

ITEM	MONTH 1	2	3	4	5	6
Product A: Price	$0	0	$20	$20	$20	$20
Product A: Units	0	0	20	45	65	85
Gross Revenue	$0	$0	$400	$900	$1,300	$1,700
Product B: Price	$0	0	$15	$15	$15	$15
Product B: Units	0	0	20	35	64	47
Gross Revenue	$0	$0	$300	$525	$960	$705
Product C: Price	$0	0	$9	$9	$9	$9
Product C: Units	0	0	30	70	90	180
Gross Revenue	$0	$0	$270	$630	$810	$1,620
Product D: Price	$0	0	$5	$5	$5	$5
Product D: Units	0	0	206	189	186	195
Gross Revenue	$0	$0	$1,030	$945	$930	$975
Grand Total	$0	$0	$2,000	$3,000	$4,000	$5,000

7	8	9	10	11	12	TOTAL
$20	$20	$20	$20	$20	$20	$20
105	143	143	170	185	198	1159
$2,100	$2,860	$2,860	$3,400	$3,700	$3,960	$23,180
$15	$15	$15	$15	$15	$15	$15
90	100	100	113	124	137	830
$1,350	$1,500	$1,500	$1,695	$1,860	$2,055	$12,450
$9	$9	$9	$9	$9	$9	$9
180	190	190	220	280	340	1770
$1,620	$1,710	$1,710	$1,980	$2,520	$3,060	$15,930
$5	$5	$5	$5	$5	$5	$5
186	186	186	185	184	185	1888
$930	$930	$930	$925	$920	$925	$9,440
$6,000	$7,000	$7,000	$8,000	$9,000	$10,000	$61,000

Exhibit 4. Blank Schedule for Cash Flow Statement

Company Name					
Proforma Statement of Cash Flows Year 1					
BEGINNING CASH BALANCE		0	0	0	0
MONTH	1	2	3	4	5
Inflows from Operations					
Base Client Sales					
Other Client Sales	0	0	0	0	0
Less: Credit Sales					
Total Cash Inflows from Current Sales	0	0	0	0	0
Plus: Collections on Prior Sales					
Total Cash Inflows from Net Sales	0	0	0	0	0
Inflows from Financing					
Equity Financing		0			
Loan	0				
Total Cash Inflows from Financing	0	0	0	0	0
TOTAL CASH INFLOWS	0	0	0	0	0
MONTH	1	2	3	4	5
Outflows from Operations:					
Employees @ 11%	0	0	0	0	0
Payroll Taxes	0	0	0	0	0
Inventory	0	0	0	0	0
Assignment Specific Supplies	0	0	0	0	0
Office Supplies	0	0	0	0	0
Postage and Overnight Delivery	0	0	0	0	0
Insurance	0	0	0	0	0
Rent					
Website					
Advertising & Promotion	0	0	0	0	0
Telephone & Utilities	0	0	0	0	0
Repairs	0	0	0	0	0
Professional Fees	0	0	0	0	0
Miscellaneous	0	0	0	0	0
Total Outflows from Operations	0	0	0	0	0
Outflows from Financing					
Loan Payments	0	0	0	0	0
Total Outflows from Financing	0	0	0	0	0
Outflows from Nonrecurring Expenses					
Fixtures & Equipment		0	0	0	0
Leasehold Improvements	0	0	0	0	0
Utility & Lease Deposits	0	0	0	0	0
Licenses & Permits	0	0	0	0	0
Total Nonrecurring Expenses	0	0	0	0	0
TOTAL OUTFLOWS	0	0	0	0	0
MONTH	1	2	3	4	5
TOTAL INFLOWS	0	0	0	0	0
TOTAL OUTFLOWS	0	0	0	0	0
NET CASH FLOWS	0	0	0	0	0
Assumptions: See attached					

0	0	0	0	0	0	0	0
6	7	8	9	10	11	12	TOTAL
							0
0	0	0	0	0	0	0	0
							0
0	0	0	0	0	0	0	0
							0
0	0	0	0	0	0	0	0
	0	0	0	0	0	0	0
							0
0	0	0	0	0	0	0	0
0	0	0	0	0	0	0	0
6	7	8	9	10	11	12	TOTAL
0	0	0	0	0	0	0	0
0	0	0	0	0	0	0	0
0	0	0	0	0	0	0	0
0	0	0	0	0	0	0	0
0	0	0	0	0	0	0	0
0	0	0	0	0	0	0	0
0	0	0	0	0	0	0	0
							0
0	0	0	0	0	0	0	0
0	0	0	0	0	0	0	0
0	0	0	0	0	0	0	0
0	0	0	0	0	0	0	0
0	0	0	0	0	0	0	0
0	0	0	0	0	0	0	0
0	0	0	0	0	0	0	0
0	0	0	0	0	0	0	0
0	0	0	0	0	0	0	0
0	0	0	0	0	0	0	0
0	0	0	0	0	0	0	0
0	0	0	0	0	0	0	0
0	0	0	0	0	0	0	0
0	0	0	0	0	0	0	0
6	7	8	9	10	11	12	TOTAL
0	0	0	0	0	0	0	
0	0	0	0	0	0	0	
0	0	0	0	0	0	0	

Exhibit 5. Schedules of Start-up Costs and Capital Budget

Start-Up Costs	MONTH 1	2	3	4	5	6	7	8	9	10	11	12	TOTAL
Occupancy Deposit	$1,000	$0	$0	$0	$0	$0	$0	$0	$0	$0	$0	$0	$1,000
Telephone Deposit	$500	$0	$0	$0	$0	$0	$0	$0	$0	$0	$0	$0	$500
Utilities Deposit	$500	$0	$0	$0	$0	$0	$0	$0	$0	$0	$0	$0	$500
Legal and Consulting/ Start-up	$2,000	$0	$0	$0	$0	$0	$0	$0	$0	$0	$0	$0	$2,000
Grand Opening/Initial Campaign	$1,000	$0	$0	$0	$0	$0	$0	$0	$0	$0	$0	$0	$1,000
Total Start-up Costs [To Sales Line on Statement of Cash Flows]	$5,000	$0	$0	$0	$0	$0	$0	$0	$0	$0	$0	$0	$5,000

Capital Budget	MONTH 1	2	3	4	5	6	7	8	9	10	11	12	TOTAL
Equipment	$7,000	$0	$0	$0	$0	$0	$0	$0	$0	$0	$0	$0	$7,000
Furniture	$2,000	$0	$0	$0	$0	$0	$0	$0	$0	$0	$0	$0	$2,000
Signage	$1,000	$0	$0	$0	$0	$0	$0	$0	$0	$0	$0	$0	$1,000
Total Capital Expenditures [To Fixtures & Equipment on Statement of Cash Flows]	$10,000	$0	$0	$0	$0	$0	$0	$0	$0	$0	$0	$0	$10,000

Exhibit 6. Blank Schedule for Units Sold and Gross Revenue

ITEM	MONTH 1	2	3	4	5	6	7	8	9	10	11	12	TOTAL
Product A: Price	$0	$0	$0	$0	$0	$0	$0	$0	$0	$0	$0	$0	$20
Product A: Units	0	0	0	0	0	0	0	0	0	0	0	0	0
Gross Revenue	$0	$0	$0	$0	$0	$0	$0	$0	$0	$0	$0	$0	$0
Product B: Price	$0	$0	$0	$0	$0	$0	$0	$0	$0	$0	$0	$0	$15
Product B: Units	0	0	0	0	0	0	0	0	0	0	0	0	0
Gross Revenue	$0	$0	$0	$0	$0	$0	$0	$0	$0	$0	$0	$0	$0
Product C: Price	$0	$0	$0	$0	$0	$0	$0	$0	$0	$0	$0	$0	$9
Product C: Units	0	0	0	0	0	0	0	0	0	0	0	0	0
Gross Revenue	$0	$0	$0	$0	$0	$0	$0	$0	$0	$0	$0	$0	$0
Product D: Price	$0	$0	$0	$0	$0	$0	$0	$0	$0	$0	$0	$0	$5
Product D: Units	0	0	0	0	0	0	0	0	0	0	0	0	0
Gross Revenue	$0	$0	$0	$0	$0	$0	$0	$0	$0	$0	$0	$0	$0
Grand Total	$0	$0	$0	$0	$0	$0	$0	$0	$0	$0	$0	$0	$0

Exhibit 7. Example of a Personal Financial Statement

IMPORTANT: Read these directions before completing this statement.

☐ If you are applying for individual credit in your own name and are relying on your own income or assets and not the income or assets of another person, as the basis for repayment of the credit requested, complete only Sections 1 and 3.

☐ If you are applying for joint credit with another person, complete sections providing information in Section 2 about applications.

☐ If you are applying for individual credit but are relying on income from alimony, child support, or separate maintenance or on the income or assets of another person as a basis for repayment of the credit requested, complete all Sections, providing information in Section 2 about the person whose alimony, support, or maintenance payments or income or assets you are relying on.

☐ If this statement relates to your guaranty of the indebtedness of other person(s), firm(s) or corporation(s), complete Sections 1 and 3.

SECTION 1—INDIVIDUAL INFORMATION (Type or Print)	SECTION 2—OTHER PARTY INFORMATION (Type or Print)
Name	Name
Residence Address	Residence Address
City, State & Zip	City, State & Zip
Position or Occupation	Position or Occupation
Business Name	Business Name
Business Address	Business Address
City, State & Zip	City, State & Zip
Res. Phone	Res. Phone

SECTION 3—STATEMENT OF FINANCIAL CONDITION AS OF _____, 20 _____

ASSETS (Do Not Include Assets of Doubtful Value)	In Dollars (Omit Cents)	LIABILITIES	In Dollars (Omit Cents)
Cash on hand and in banks		Notes payable to banks—secured	
U.S. Gov't & Marketable Securities—see Schedule A		Notes payable to banks—unsecured	
Nonmarketable Securities—see Schedule B		Due to brokers	
Securities held by broker in margin accounts		Amount payable to others—secured	
Restricted or control stocks		Amount payable to others—unsecured	
Partial Interest in Real Estate Equities—see Schedule C		Accounts and bills due	
		Unpaid income tax	
Real Estate Owned—see Schedule D		Other unpaid taxes and interest	
Loans Receivable		Real estate mortgages payable—see Schedule D	
Automobiles and other personal property			
Cash value-life insurance—see Schedule E		Other debts—itemize:	
Other assets—itemize:			
		TOTAL LIABILITIES	
		NET WORTH	
TOTAL ASSETS		TOTAL LIABILITIES AND NET WORTH	

SOURCES OF INCOME FOR THE YEAR ENDED _____, 20_____		PERSONAL INFORMATION
Salary bonuses & commissions	$	Do you have a will? _____ If so, name the executor.
Dividends		
Real estate Income		Are you a partner or officer in any other venture? If so, describe.
Other Income (alimony, child support, or separate maintenance income need not be revealed if you do not wish to have it considered as a basis for repaying this obligation)		Are you obligated to pay alimony, child support or separate maintenance payments? If so, describe.
PLEASE ATTACH A COPY OF YOUR MOST RECENT INCOME TAX RETURN		
		Are any assets pledged other than as described on schedules? If so, describe.
TOTAL	$	
CONTINGENT LIABILITIES		
Do you have any contingent liabilities? If so, describe.		Income tax settled through (date)_____
		Are you a defendant in any suits or legal actions?

As endorser, or maker or guarantor?	$	Personal bank accounts carried at:
On leases or contracts?	$	
Legal claims	$	
Other special debt	$	Have you ever been declared bankrupt?
Amount of contested income tax liens	$	If so, describe.

SCHEDULE A—U.S. GOVERNMENT & MARKETABLE SECURITIES

Number of Shares of Face Value (Bonds)	Description	In Name of	Are These Pledged	Market Value

SCHEDULE B—NONMARKETABLE SECURITIES

Number of Shares	Description	In Name of	Are These Pledged	Source of Value	Value

SCHEDULE C—PARTIAL INTEREST IN REAL ESTATE EQUITIES

Address & Type of Property	Title in Name of	% of Ownership	Date Acquired	Cost	Market Value	Mortgage Maturity	Mortgage Amount

SCHEDULE D—REAL ESTATE OWNED

Address & Type of Property	Title in Name of	Date Acquired	Cost	Market Value	Mortgage Maturity	Mortgage Amount

SCHEDULE E—LIFE INSURANCE CARRIED, INCLUDING N.S.L.I. AND GROUP INSURANCE

Name of Insurance Company	Owner of Policy	Beneficiary	Face Amount	Policy Loans	Cash Surrender Value

SCHEDULE F—BANKS OR FINANCE COMPANIES WHERE CREDIT HAS BEEN OBTAINED

Name and Address of Lender	Credit in the Name of	Secured or Unsecured	Original Date	High Credit	Current Balance

The information contained in the statement is provided for the purpose of obtaining, or maintaining credit with you on behalf of the undersigned, or persons, firms or corporations in whose behalf the undersigned may either severally or jointly with others, execute a guaranty in your favor. Each undersigned understands that you are relying on the information provided herein (including the designation made as to ownership of property) in deciding to grant or continue credit. Each undersigned represents and warrants that the information provided is true and complete and that you may consider this statement as continuing to be true and correct until a written notice of a change is given to you by the undersigned. You are authorized to make all inquiries you deem necessary to verify the accuracy of the statements made herein, and to determine my/our creditworthiness. You are authorized to answer questions about your credit experience with me/us.

Date Signed _____, 20 _____

Signature (Individual) _____

S.S. No._____

Signature (Other Party)_____

S.S. No._____

INDEX

Index

Index

Index

Index